Dear John:

This is an unassuming little tract, but its arrival will serve to remind you of my enduring appreciation for your interest in my work.

George K.

Princeton,
 4 Oct., 2000

AN AMERICAN FAMILY

An
AMERICAN
FAMILY

The Kennans

The First Three Generations

GEORGE F. KENNAN

W. W. NORTON & COMPANY
New York · London

Copyright © 2000 by George F. Kennan

For information about permission to reproduce selections from
this book, write to Permissions, W. W. Norton & Company, Inc.,
500 Fifth Avenue, New York, NY 10110

The text of this book is composed in 11/15.25 Caslon Regular
with the display set in Caslon Italic and Caslon Expert Regular
Composition by Sue Carlson
Manufacturing by The Maple-Vail Book Manufacturing Group
Book design by Charlotte Staub
Photographic research by Brandon Griggs

Library of Congress Cataloging-in-Publication Data

Kennan, George Frost, 1904–
An American family : the Kennans—the first three generations /
George F. Kennan.
     p.   cm.
Includes bibliographical references.
ISBN 0-393-05034-3
1. Kennan family. 2. Kennan, George Frost, 1904—Family.
3. New England—Biography. I. Title.
CT274.K45 K46 2000
974'.04'0922dc21
[B]   00-032910

W. W. Norton & Company, Inc., 500 Fifth Avenue, New York,
N.Y. 10110
www.wwnorton.com

W. W. Norton & Company Ltd., 10 Coptic Street, London
WC1A 1PU

1 2 3 4 5 6 7 8 9 0

CONTENTS

LIST OF
Illustrations AND *Maps*

This book has been written for the benefit of my children and their descendants in the hope that it may stimulate in their hearts a love for the ties of kindred, and for the memory of worthy ancestors. I hope it will serve to arouse their curiosity concerning the remoter authors of their existence, and induce them to study the character and habits of the founders of this great Republic as represented in their own ancestry.

It is hoped that this feeble effort to retrieve from oblivion something of the history and genealogy of the Kennan family will serve as the beginning of a work which will be followed up and added to by my descendants from generation to generation.

—Thomas Lathrop Kennan, in his preface
to *Genealogy of the Kennan Family*, 1907

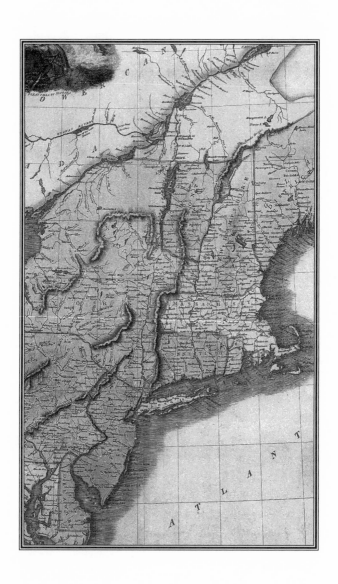

ACKNOWLEDGMENTS

here are three persons whose contributions to this volume have been of such exceptional importance that they deserve special mention. They are:

My Princeton friend, Sir John Thomson, a native of the Dumfries region, who gave me valuable help in establishing the identities of the antecedents of the first American Kennan;

Mrs. Mary Hutchins Lindow, of Chile, Wisconsin, for her patient consultations and for her remarkable privately printed study entitled *Lest We Forget Our Pioneer Heritage;*

and

Ms. Mary Bull, of Boston, for her spontaneous and most effective explorations, on behalf of this study, of the eighteenth-century history and environment of Charlemont, Massachusetts.

To both of these women, this writer's heart goes out. And it goes out also to the librarians who have given invariably quiet and self-effacing help at a number of places, outstanding among them the New England Historic Genealogical Society, the great genealogical section of the New York Public Library, and the Speer Library at the Princeton Theological

Seminary. As one who regards its library culture as probably the greatest of this country's contributions to world culture, help from that quarter has had a special meaning for me.

AN AMERICAN FAMILY
The Kennans'
First Three Generations

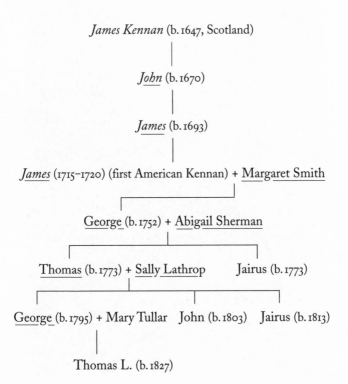

James Kennan (b. 1647, Scotland)
|
John (b. 1670)
|
James (b. 1693)
|
James (1715–1720) (first American Kennan) + Margaret Smith

George (b. 1752) + Abigail Sherman

Thomas (b. 1773) + Sally Lathrop   Jairus (b. 1773)

George (b. 1795) + Mary Tullar   John (b. 1803)   Jairus (b. 1813)

Thomas L. (b. 1827)

y honored grandfather, Thomas Lathrop Kennan, Wisconsin "old settler," Civil War veteran, and country attorney, decided in the years of his retirement from active affairs to interest himself in the genealogy of the paternal line of our family. To this end he undertook a number of investigations, and produced, in 1907, a small and privately printed volume entitled *Genealogy of the Kennan Family.** This was a purely genealogical record, listing the names and interrelationships of the male members of the family, departing from the family's first appearance in North America in the early eighteenth century and carrying it down to the end of the nineteenth century. As such, it was of unique value to any interested descendants. And indeed, without it the following study could scarcely have been undertaken at all. But it was, by intention, strictly factual, devoid of interpretive or critical comment, and devoid, too, of treatment of the human, geographic, or historical backgrounds of the events mentioned.

In undertaking and completing this work, Grand-

*Thomas Lathrop Kennan, *Genealogy of the Kennan Family* (Milwaukee: Cannon Printing Co., 1907).

father was, as already noted, no longer young—was in his seventies, in fact. It was thus not unnatural that the writer of these lines, having attained an even greater age, should have returned with renewed respect and sympathy to his grandfather's work and have asked himself whether there was not something that could be done to broaden and make more vivid the image of these earlier members of the family whose identities Grandfather had been at such pains to establish. What would be here required would not be any further genealogical research but something rather in the nature of an actual family history. And it was also clear that for a number of personal reasons the preparation of such a history could never be (and has in fact to date never been) more than a leisure-time hobby.

Recognizing this limitation, I did, however, apply myself to the task of preparing material for such a study wherever the possibilities presented themselves. But there came a point at which, by force of circumstances, this effort had to be put aside. And not knowing whether I would ever be able to resume it, and perceiving the danger that what little I had by that time learned might, unless in some way preserved, be lost entirely, I put together in a summary paper the results of my efforts up to that time, had them privately printed in a small volume entitled *An American Kennan Family 1744–1913,* and made it available to a small circle of family members and friends.

Not long thereafter, however, fortune took a more favorable turn. So I was then able to return to the work and to give it all that age, time, and strength permitted. The result was the volume that follows. But I think I should make it clear, at least for those who may have seen the smaller and more preliminary volume just referred to, that in preparing this present volume I have not hesitated to draw freely upon its small predecessor wherever this seemed suitable, and this without specific reference to it.

Beyond that, there are two important respects in which what I am now writing differs not only from what was set forth in the earlier volume but from what other scholars might well consider to be the permissible limits of historical effort. I have, in the first place, taken account here not only of such events as appeared *provable* by documentary evidence, but also of such others as seemed sufficiently *probable* to deserve mention.

And then, secondly, I have, where I thought it relevant, included my own intuitive feelings for the backgrounds of particularly obscure or baffling episodes.

In risking these departures from the stricter rules of historical writing, I have had in mind that most works of history tend to be no less revealing for the mental and aesthetic world of the author than for the subjects of which he treats. Particularly is this the case when the subject is the history of the author's own family. So, while I recognize that to take the liberties just referred to may be seen by some as dealing too roughly with the fine details of the story, I also feel that this adds color and perspective to the story as a whole. And this, for the average prospective reader, is what is most important.

AN AMERICAN FAMILY

Public record of marriage on May 25, 1744,
of James McKennan and Margaret Smith.

INTRODUCTION

n addressing this volume to readers young and old, I am acutely aware that younger ones are not likely to have much interest in the subject with which it deals. And although genealogy is normally of greater interest to the old than to the young, not even all older readers may experience much curiosity about this bit of it. But there may be exceptions. Those who are now young will someday be older. It may then occur to them, too, as it has to so many older people, that we are all participants in continuities linking the genes and experiences of our forefathers with those of our own lifetimes, and that such is the importance of inheritance and tradition in the determination of personality that without some knowledge of one's antecedents—of the conditions that formed them and of the ways in which they tended to react to those conditions—one will always be lacking in the ability (limited even in the best of circumstances) to understand oneself.

I must stress at once that this is a genealogical history only of the *Kennan* line. For each of the generations there was, of course, also a female line, that of the respective wife and mother, which was of a genetic and cultural importance no smaller than that of the Ken-

nan line. The importance of the female lines is evident
from the fact that only some 3 percent of my own
genetic inheritance would seem to have been derived,
statistically at least, from the first Kennan to have
arrived on North American soil, the remainder being
largely from the various families into which Kennans,
in the ensuing generations, intermarried. Genetically
speaking, we today are just as much the descendants
of a Margaret Smith, an Abigail Sherman, a Sally
Lathrop, and a Mary Tullar, as we are of that first Kennan ancestor. And if we extend the view to include not
only these women themselves but also the genetic
inheritance each of them brought with her, as one
would be well justified in doing, we would have to
bring in several other families as well. All of the ladies
were of English origin. All seem to have had firm
roots, incidentally, in the very earliest settlers of sev-
enteenth-century colonial New England. So, if genetic inheritance were everything, what sort of Scots
would we Kennans now be?

It may be asked: why then write about just the
Kennans?

A logical question; but there are answers. First, I
had Grandfather Kennan's book as a starter. In respect
to none of the other families did I have any such foun-
dation to build on. To have tried to pursue each of
these female lines as intensely as the Kennan line
would have required an amount of time and travel I
simply could not have given to it.

Yet beyond all that, some paternal genes do seem to
be relatively persistent and enduring. And there does
seem to be such a thing as tradition—a tradition mod-
ified and supplemented, to be sure, by each of the
wives that married into the family, but not wholly

negated by any of them. Besides which, habit and religion, always partly shared among the generations, were powerful factors in the shaping of personality, much more powerful in those earlier generations, in fact, than they are today.

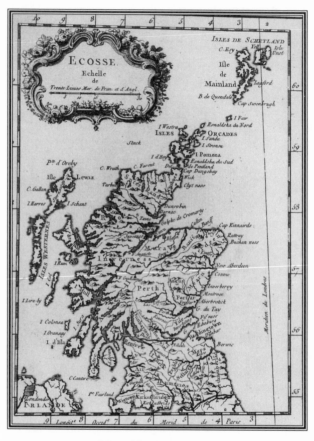

Map of Scotland, c. 1800.

ONE

The Scottish Background

very genealogical table must necessarily be based on the arbitrary choice of some figure, usually dim, and often mythical, to serve as the patriarch, or occasionally the matriarch, from whom the family line is conceived as taking off. The farther back the choice reaches, the dimmer and less meaningful becomes the selection. But for our purposes it should do, I think, to accept, as the first reasonably identifiable patriarch of our Kennan family, one James Kennan, born in 1647 in the town of Dumfries in southwestern Scotland—a town in which he passed his life and where he died in 1691.

Dumfries was then a very small town by our standard. Even in the middle of the twentieth century, it had only some thirty thousand residents, and it must have been smaller still two or three centuries earlier. But it was the administrative seat of three of the old counties of southwestern Scotland, and the most important center of that entire region. It was very strongly, indeed almost exclusively, Presbyterian-Protestant. In the wake of the religious wars of the earlier part of the seventeenth century, this was a factor of great importance.

The town seems to have included no aristocratic or patrician families in the accepted European usage of those terms. Dominant in the town council of the early eighteenth century were the merchants, the local clergy, and the remaining members of the old medieval handicraft guilds. The leading officials were the burgess (the mayor), the "bailie" (or bailiff, who served as town executive and chief of police), and the magistrates of the local court, who presumably had primarily a juridical function. The burgesses, appointed by the Town Council, served for a term of only one year.

Our patriarchal James Kennan was plainly a prominent man about town. He served at one time or another both as burgess and as bailie. In the later years of his life he represented the town, and indeed the entire region, as commissioner to the Scottish parliament in Edinburgh. But beyond that, I know nothing of his person. He was referred to, in a history of Dumfries written in 1746, as "an old Cromwellian," which presumably meant that he had, in the confused religious wars of then recent memory, fought alongside the Cromwellian forces. But if he did, it is reasonable to suspect that it was for restricted and specifically Scottish goals rather than for those of the English Cromwell that he fought.

The "lawful son and heir" of James Kennan was one John of that name. He was born, we must assume, somewhere around 1670. He, too, seems to have had a prominent place in the Dumfries community, occupying at some point the position of bailie. And he seems to have had a number of sons, the first of whom, another James, dutifully named after his grandfather, was born in 1693, the remaining births stringing along until 1709. Is it permissible to suspect that this second James was the father of a third one who, born somewhere around the years 1715–1720, emigrated to New England and became the first of the American Kennans?

The best that my own grandfather was able to do in establishing the identity of this first American Kennan was to note that in 1744, in either Rutland or Holden, Massachusetts, two colonial villages not far from Worcester, a man by the name of James Kennan married a girl by the name of Margaret Smith. Grandfather suspected, I believe, that the man in question had had some connection with a family in Dumfries, but he was not able to find what this connection was. Today, with certain of the Dumfries records before us, and particularly when we look at the first names of the sons that were to proceed from this Kennan-Smith marriage of 1744,* it becomes quite clear that the relationship described above was indeed in all probability the true one. But the question still remains: how and why did this young man, a James Kennan born in Dumfries at some time in the period 1715–1720, find himself so far from home and entering upon this marriage at the time and place in question?

The first and almost the only clue we have to the

---

*The first of the sons of this marriage was given, quite properly and customarily, the name of the paternal grandfather, John. The second was given the name George, that having been the name of a little brother of James who had died in infancy. (It was common practice at that time when one child had died that way to give the name to one born later.) A third son received the name Andrew, that of James's older brother.

answer is one that relates to his bride, Margaret Smith. We do know something of *her* origin, and of what brought her to New England. To explain the nature of this clue requires a certain digression, one that takes us to northern Ireland, the part of Ireland now commonly known as Ulster.

For many years in the past, at that time, it had been common for young Scots, particularly ones from southwestern Scotland who found life in Scotland hard going, to emigrate to Ulster, a region separated from southwestern Scotland only by a strait some twenty miles in width. Most of these seem to have been sheep farmers and weavers of linen; these, at any rate, were the occupations which many of them, once in Ulster, pursued.

As the eighteenth century began, conditions in that part of Ireland became extremely difficult for these Scots. The reasons for this were primarily economic but also religious. The result was a heavy flow of Scottish migration, continuing over much of the eighteenth century, from Ulster to the New World, and primarily to North America. In later decades, this movement was mainly directed to and through the ports of Philadelphia and New York, but it was largely inaugurated in the years 1718 to 1721 by the arrival at the port of Boston of several hundred of these people, carried in the holds of thirty or forty of the small ships of that day. About the further fate of these people, after their arrival in Boston, little information seems to be available. One body of them endeavored to settle in the vicinity of Worcester, Massachusetts, where they were hostilely received by the long-established English colonial settlers, and whence, presumably, they dispersed to other parts of New England; but there is no evidence that our Kennan ancestor was among them.

Now, the reason for this digression is that on the passenger list of one of the first of these shiploads of Scottish emigrants from Ulster to Boston, we find the names of a James and Margaret Smith and their daughter Margaret, the latter evidently at that time an infant. And because it was apparently this daughter who, twenty-six years later, was to become the bride of our first American Kennan ancestor, the question at once presents itself: could not the bridegroom James, too, have been one of these young Scots who emigrated first to Ulster and thence, at some time between 1718 and 1721, on another of those first ships, to Boston?

This is an attractive suggestion, and one that would explain the connection between the two families. But for various reasons, the first being that there is simply no proof of it or any hard suggestive evidence to support it, we cannot accept it. Even if there were some sort of evidence, it would raise more questions than it would answer. Our James is unlikely to have been more than thirty years old or less than eighteen to twenty when he married, in which case he could not have been more than seven years old at the time of the arrival of even the last of these particular ships. Moreover, Grandfather tells us (and there is other evidence of it) that James, at or around the time of his marriage, was the owner of a farm in the neighborhood of Holden. But when and how could he have acquired such a farm? He, a young boy without agricultural experience, could not have built it with his own hands in the years before his marriage to Margaret Smith in 1744.

If he really came to New England in his boyhood,

even if in the years just after 1721, James would, one may suppose, have come in the company of some older person. But who could that have been? There were, except for the Smiths, almost no other Scots in the Rutland–Holden area.* One is reduced, in the end, to speculation on two hypotheses: (1) that he was brought to Massachusetts, and in some way installed in the Rutland–Holden area, by someone of whose identity we have no inkling; and/or (2) that he was not poor but came to Massachusetts reasonably well-heeled and bought the farm he was understood, by my grandfather, to have owned. Of these two hypotheses (which are not mutually exclusive), the second would seem to have the greater plausibility. After all, the Kennan family in Dumfries was itself not all that poor. And some twenty-six years later, when James moved (as we shall see) to another part of Massachusetts, he seems to have been involved in the acquisition of farming property of considerable market value.

We are left, then, with the first definitely ascertainable fact about the American branch of the Kennan family, which was the marriage, in the year 1744, in or near the village of Holden, not far from Worcester, Massachusetts. How were that place and that date to be related to the political and administrative realities of the time?

Massachusetts had by this time been an English colony for approximately a century. Another thirty-

---

*Among some three hundred inscriptions on the gravestones of that period in the old Rutland cemetery one finds, in addition to that of one of the Smith family, only two Scottish ones; and neither of these would qualify as the final resting place of anyone who could possibly have been the companion of the young Kennan.

four years were to elapse before it would become, first, independent, and then, some years later, one of the founding states of the American Union. During this entire colonial period the governmental arrangements, especially those that affected the towns and villages, were, in the first place, far from being uniform throughout the entire Commonwealth; and they were in an almost constant state of change and revision as human settlement spread across the region. The government of the colonial Commonwealth, at its Boston center, was headed, of course, by the governor; but included a General Court, a body largely of local American composition, which exercised administrative authority over Massachusetts as a whole. Below that, there were the various local authorities of counties, towns, villages, and farming areas. These latter authorities embraced many features of elected self-government, the qualification for citizenship in the town being normally the possession of a modest amount of property, monetary or otherwise. But the church, too, had its role to play, and in part a secular one, in the small communities. And to this pattern it should be added that the farther a small community was distanced from the major administrative centers of the Commonwealth, the greater its freedom to design its own practices and meet local requirements. This was very much the case in the rural vicinity the Kennans were now to inhabit.

It was to all this, then, that this Kennan family had to adjust their lives on the farm near Holden. One of the first tests to which this put them must have been to find a pastor to marry the first parents. There appears then to have been no regular church in Holden, the nearest one being the Congregational church in the town of Rutland, some six miles distant. The pastor of that was a man named Buckminister, who had only recently taken over that position, his predecessor having been killed by the Indians several years earlier.

The figure of the Rev. Mr. Buckminister endeared itself to me some time ago in the reading of an anecdote about his personality (I have now forgotten where). He, it seems, finding himself on one occasion addressed by a parishioner in a manner he found disrespectful, flung at the latter, in the phraseology of that day, the equivalent of the more modern challenge "Who do you think you're talking to?" To which the parishioner hurled back: "To a poor worm of the dust, like myself." To which the pastor responded by burying his face in his hands and saying: "Ah, I know it, I know it."

Buckminister must, in any case, have been a man eminently acceptable to the local community as its spiritual leader, for he served a total of fifty years in that capacity. What brought him to Holden to perform the Kennan marriage we do not know; but this was a fully proper procedure, Holden being already the home of the bride's parents, and James Kennan the suitor. But it is also evident that the pastor required, as a condition for his conduct of the marriage service, that the bridegroom's father become a member of his Rutland church and purchase a private pew in that structure, which James Kennan promptly did. (We have no evidence, however, that the family ever lived in Rutland.)

On the farm near Holden the life of the family proceeded over the course of some twenty-six years. During that period the wife, Margaret, gave birth to nine or ten children, of whom all but one survived the diseases of early childhood common in those rural regions. All these children, we must suppose, went at one time or another to the local village school in Holden. But beyond that, we know nothing, other than ownership of the church pew in Rutland, about the social life or other personal connections of the family. The only evidence we have of the educational level of the parents strongly suggests that the mother was illiterate. (Later in life, when obliged to sign a legal document, she simply "made her mark.") This, of course, in the circumstances, says nothing about her qualities as a wife and a mother. The husband must be supposed to have received a decent schooling either before departure from Dumfries or wherever else he lived through his growing years; but there is no evidence of anything beyond that. Nor do his intellectual horizons appear ever to have risen beyond the life of a farmer.

At the end of these twenty-six years of residence in the vicinity of Worcester, in the east-central part of Massachusetts, James Kennan and his family abandoned the Holden farm and moved some forty-five miles further west, to the vicinity of the small and relatively new town of Charlemont in the northwestern part of the state, not far from the present Vermont border.

Both the reasons for this move and its consequences will be the subject of the next chapter.

A map of Charlemont, Massachusetts, dated 1780, shows the exact location of the Kennan farm.

TWO

Charlemont

harlemont, although officially recognized as a town, was in reality, in the 1770s, still a village. It was pleasantly situated on the banks of the Deerfield River, as this stream pursued its peaceful way from the high hills of northwestern Massachusetts to its juncture with the great Connecticut River and thence to the sea.

Driving with my wife up to northern Massachusetts in the spring of 1968, I recalled what my grandfather had written in his book on the family, composed some sixty years before that time, about the family's life in Charlemont in the eighteenth century; and, finding that our route (to a son's commencement) brought us not too far from that place, I decided to stop off there for a day to see whether there could now be unearthed from the modern Charlemont something more about the family's residence there in the years 1773 to 1792 than what grandfather had brought to light.

So this we did. And it now occurs to me that there

might be a worse way of introducing a small chapter on Charlemont in this present exercise than to quote parts of a letter written shortly thereafter to my sister Jeanette, describing that visit to the place in June of 1968.

So we set off on Tuesday evening, driving through New York, Hartford, and Springfield—stopping overnight at one of those motels where the roar of traffic on the highway never stops all night (I discovered in the morning that in addition to the big highway we were on, we were right under the Massachusetts Turnpike, and next to a huge air force base). In addition, the place was so modern that there was no openable window (a prized achievement of modern architecture), and of course the air-conditioning did not work, so I had to prop the door open, preferring thieves to suffocation, and I slept little.

In early morning I turned on the TV and learned of the shooting of Bobby Kennedy. Although we had not supported him, it was a real shock and source of sadness to us both. In the motel coffee shop, where we breakfasted, all we patrons sat glumly avoiding each other's eyes, as though we were ashamed of something—as in a sense we were.

However, life must go on. So we pursued our way, in the loveliest sort of weather, and arrived at Charlemont by 10:00 A.M. I don't know whether you have seen the place. The Deerfield River flows east, at that point, between hills. The valley is relatively narrow, and what there is of bottomland, created no doubt by the meanderings of the river and the alluvial deposits, is so scanty that there is scarcely room for more than one farm, and sometimes even less than that, each side of the river. It was presumably on one or more of these farms that

the McKennan* family settled when they moved
there about 1770. The town of Charlemont itself is
strung out along the road—the Mohawk Trail—
that leads along the north bank of the river.

Our first visit was to the very un-New-Englandish red-brick town hall—a small structure built in
the middle of the last century. It was labeled as the
library, and did indeed contain the town library; but
the latter was closed. The only room open was the
relief office, where there sat a young woman, also
very un-New-Englandish, who acknowledged that
she was "not from here," and knew no one who
could be suspected of having any knowledge of the
history of the place. She did, however, tell me that
the librarian usually came in on Wednesday after-
noons; and when I pointed out to her, to her apparent surprise, that this was Wednesday, she admitted
that I might have a chance to encounter the librarian if she came back later.

I then repaired to the inn, to phone the librarian. A sign on the inn said it had been built in 1787.
This was, presumably, some five or six years before
the removal of most of the family from
Charlemont; and I had my moment of the historian's excitement from the reflection that my great-
great-great-grandfather George had no doubt
witnessed its erection, and perhaps (since he later
"kept hotel" in Waterbury) been involved in it. It
was a cool, dark structure, roomy and slightly shab-
by inside. In the big living room, two women—one

*The first American generation of Kennans used the Scottish
patronymic "Mc," though it was rarely, if ever, used in Dumfries,
and after an occasional use by one of James's sons in the
Charlemont period, it seems to have been dropped entirely.
James may have used it to distinguish himself from the Irish
Catholic Keenans.

a young woman lying on a sofa and looking unwell—were watching TV for the news of the events in Los Angeles. The older woman, the proprietress, talked loudly and harshly, with a western accent, and was also obviously "not from there." She, like everyone else I met that day, hadn't been for R. Kennedy and "hadn't particularly liked him" but felt it was a terrible thing he'd been shot and wondered what the country was coming to. This, she said, was one of the times when she was glad she lived "in a little hick town like this" and not in one of the great cities.

The librarian was said to be coming in at 2:30. There seemed to be no other favorable place to turn in Charlemont proper, that morning. But I recalled reading in a history of Charlemont (discovered in the Princeton University library) that the town had had, around the time of the Revolution, no church of its own, the church having been situated somewhat further north, at a place called Heath. We set out, therefore, up the road to that place. The road wound up and up into the hills, through dense forest, following the course of a lovely rushing mountain stream. Some six miles above Charlemont, at an elevation of 1,650 feet, we came out into an upland clearing, on which was the village of Heath—a place of perhaps some ten or twelve houses. I stopped at one which had the post office sign on it. Actually, the post office occupied only one tiny little room. There, apparently at leisure, sat the postmistress, a large, dark-haired woman in young middle age, somewhat startled to see a stranger, hence cautious at first, assuming the characteristic country deadpan, but shrewd and not unkind. She couldn't help me much. The old church had been torn down in the middle of the last century. She didn't know where its records had

gone. The wood from it had been used for the little building (she pointed to it through the window
across the meadowlike common) that they were
now fixing up for an "historical building"—a local
museum of sorts. She had no idea where the old
records would be. But there was a lady—a Mrs.
Austin—who lived further up the hill, beyond the
present church, and who interested herself in
genealogy. Perhaps she could tell us something.

Up the hill we went. The house beyond the
church was a fine old New England house, squar-
ish and with a white clapboard exterior which
needed paint. It stood in isolation, and the surrounding grass wanted cutting. A wooden sign
showed the date of construction as 1790. The
doorstep was made of two great stones, the lower
one of which, semicircular, must have weighed several hundred pounds.

The occupant—the sole occupant, by all appear-
ances—was a tall, grayed lady, who chattered away
at us, apologizing for her appearance and for that of
the living room, and even continued to chatter
while she disappeared into the wings to change her
skirt. The room itself—like that of the inn—had a
certain dim, dingy spaciousness. The floorboards
were at least a foot wide, and the whole place had
that feeling and smell of old wood, slight damp-
ness, and faded hangings that you get in old houses without central heat. A large Franklin stove
dominated the living room.

Our hostess was obviously pressing to get away,
so we excused ourselves. She told us, as we left, that
the house was for sale—it was too big for her, etc.
But I repressed the temptation to become the
owner of more real estate (it *was* a temptation, for
the site, there on the upland "heath," was idyllic),
and we pursued our way.

On the way down to the valley we took one or
two side excursions on foot into the little side roads,
to walk the dog. Dense woods, and one or two
abandoned houses. One lovely place with a
millpond—a dammed pond, at least, and below it a
thirty-foot waterfall. Along the little stream, on the
other side from the road, there wound a wagon
track. On such a track, I thought, our ancestors
must have wended their way up the hill to church,
if that was where they really went.

Lunch at the inn, in the cool dark barroom. The
TV regaled us, from its corner, with a combination
of bulletins about the assassination and the dying
Kennedy, on the one hand, and some idiotic guess-
ing show, on the other: a bit for everyone—a bit for
the broken-hearted and a bit for the moron.

There was a half hour or so to be passed, after
lunch, before we could go to the library; and we
used it to visit the big graveyard along the road,
near town. But it went back only to the early nineteenth century, and there were no Kennan graves.
The librarian, too, was an amiable but confused old
woman, of little help. The volume of vital statistics
(not that it would have contained anything new)
was missing; and there was no history of
Charlemont—she even asked me to send her the
data on the one I had seen in Princeton.

The day was wearing on, and we were due in
Groton in the evening, so I gave up the quest at that
point. But on the way to Groton, I stopped in
Greenfield, at the courthouse, and looked, briefly
and hastily, into the old deeds for that part of the
country. They were in beautiful shape: photostated,
bound, and carefully indexed. Most of the ones I
saw were the same ones Grandpa Kennan had
seen—only one or two differences. [There was a
deed bearing Margaret Kennan's "mark," as men-

tioned above.] Her boys, on the other hand, all signed. And our ancestor George was even shown, in 1788, as collector of Charlemont and selling for some twenty shillings a bit of property on which someone had failed to pay his taxes. Also, I learned a little more about where he lived—in 1777, at least.

It is obvious that if any conclusions are to be drawn from this, my first visit to Charlemont, one of them is that one cannot expect the denizens of any place at any time to be greatly informed or interested in the doings of people who inhabited that place a couple of hundred years before they came along. For this, the preoccupation with the present, which always seems to contemporaries to be the highest and most important passage in world history, is too compelling. This being the case, the historian is left to fall back primarily on the surviving physical relics, documentary or epistolary, of the time in question. And they rarely tell the whole story.

What drew the attention of James Kennan and his family to Charlemont and induced them to move to that place remains a matter of conjecture. The agricultural advantages of such a move have already been mentioned. There was already in existence, not far from Charlemont, a small community of just such Scots as were the Kennans—a place called Colrain; and urgings from that quarter presumably played a part. The move, in any case, was not a particularly arduous one—only some forty-five miles, four or five days' journey with horse-drawn equipment.

Father Kennan, in any case, seems to have concluded, or have been on the point of concluding, just at the time of the move, a deal with a man by the name (so understood at least by my grandfather) of Warren

Booth (my own inquiry reveals that the first name was not Warren but Aaron—a mistake easily made in an age when so much communication was oral rather than written) for the joint purchase and operation of a good-sized riverside farm, not far from the town of Charlemont. One can well picture the father, with this in view, looking eagerly ahead to a new period in the family's life, centered on a new and more ample habitation than Holden had been able to provide, and this on a richer and stronger farm, with five stout sons to contribute the labor.

But if these were the father's dreams, reality seems to have dealt brutally with them. For the change turned out to produce, over the ensuing years, not the family's unity and strength but its disintegration.

The reasons for this were various. Mr. Booth, a resident of central Connecticut, was suddenly confronted at just this time with a compelling family crisis in the form of the fatal illness and death of his wife, still in Connecticut, obliging him to give up all idea of acquiring a farm in the Charlemont area. He disappeared abruptly, in any case, from the local scene, never again to appear as a coowner of the farm, despite the fact that the original purchase had evidently been officially recorded in both their names. Either James Kennan must have bought him out, or, as seems more likely, there had originally been two approximately equal parcels of land, probably side by side, one marked for Kennan and the other for Booth, and that the latter simply sold his parcel to an outsider and the coownership was liquidated. (There will be a bit more about this in the next chapter).

What now remained, in any case, for the Kennans to occupy was a curiously narrow and elongated strip of land in a north-south orientation, the southern end meeting the river. It consisted of fifty-one acres of what must have been excellent farm land, and supported at least one fair-sized farmhouse.

A second surprising change in the family's situation occurred when George, one of the five sons, suddenly, and at just the time of the family's move, having been sent together with his father as an advance party to prepare for the arrival of the others, met, wooed, and married a young woman whose identity and fate will be treated in the next chapter. And, as though that were not enough, the marriage was shortly to be followed, in June 1773, by the birth of the first of their children. This removed him from further residence in the family circles.

And finally, as though all this were not enough in the way of surprises, only some two to three years after the family's arrival at its new home, the Revolutionary War broke out, and four of the five sons, all but George, were either called or volunteered for military service, sometimes on repeated occasions, during the period of April 1775 to September 1777. Such help as they could have given to the father over those years, and others, must have been, at best, episodic. And in these circumstances, the main burden of operation of the farm must have been shared between the father and his son George. And since father James, now rapidly approaching the time of his own death, may have been in a state of declining health and strength, a great deal of the burden must have come to rest on the shoulders of George.

We do not know where George and his now rapidly expanding family actually lived over this period. But that a large and growing share of his time and energy must have had to do with the operation of the farm is something that flows so clearly from the known circumstances that we have no choice but to accept it.

The father's death, in any case, seems clearly to have occurred at some time during, or around, the year 1779. We have never discovered where he was buried. His widow, the simple Scottish-born Margaret Smith, survived him. She inherited, we learn from the legal documents, one third of the value of the farm; and the last we learn of her is that at the end of some ten years after her husband's death, she was still living somewhere in or around Charlemont and eking out an existence as a "spinner."

This is as good a place as any to take note, not without sadness, of how little we really know about father James Kennan. We know, with reasonable assurance, where and when he was born in Scotland, and into what sort of a family. We know where and when he first popped up on the written records of this country. We know where and when he was married, and where, for some twenty-six years, he farmed in the Worcester region. But we know nothing of him personally. Circumstantial evidence supports the conclusion that he was a man of sound principles with a strong sense of duty, a good and faithful husband, and a firm but caring father. He must have known, as he died, that he had given to his children all that his means, his insights, and his efforts could afford; and I suspect that he was well pleased with, and perhaps proud of, the results.

With one minor exception, James Kennan appears to have taken no part in the local public affairs of the Charlemont community. The exception was a brief period of service on the wartime internal security commission of the town of Charlemont. Since no one in Charlemont seems to have known him personally, this appointment was probably given to him in recognition of the services tendered to the Revolutionary cause by his four sons.

But before we leave entirely the account of James Kennan and his farm, we ought, I think, to note (and the recognition of it is important in more connotations than just this one) that the location of the farm at the very southeastern corner of the Charlemont township, while it made James a citizen of the township, did not automatically make him a citizen of the town. The region surrounding the Kennan farm was actually a part of a rapidly developing smaller community coming to be known as East Charlemont. While its distance from the Charlemont center was no more than about five miles, it would be wrong to think of this in terms of the modern suburban relationship. There was no communication between the two places other than by foot, on horseback, or by horse-drawn wagon—sometimes, in winter, there was scarcely any communication at all. The smaller community was too far away to permit its children to attend the Charlemont center's schools; and East Charlemont, at the time we are considering, was just at the point of developing, albeit in complete accord with the center, its own school.

Nor was this all that set it off from the center. Given its situation, there was much confusion over the accepted borders of two other townships: those of Buckland, to the south, and of Colrain, to the northeast. At the time when the Kennans occupied their farm, and indeed as late as 1785, Buckland, across the river, was still claiming that land for its own. And although the claim did not stand up, and the counter-claims of Charleton were soon recognized and have proved to be enduring, one can see that the region of the farm was still far away, in more than one sense, from what people have thought of as the town of Charlemont.

All this being the case, it is not surprising that the members of James Kennan's family had little sense of affiliation with that town, and that the passage of the family through its vicinity over the years of James Kennan's life left so few traces in the records of that town itself.

A somewhat different case now presents itself, however, in that of his son George and in the period after father James's death. And to that picture we must now turn.

Phoebe Denison, who married Gibson Harris of Norwich, Conn., a son of Samuel Harris and they had a son named

George Harris who married Sarah Hubbard, a daughter of Isaac Hubbard. They had a daughter named

Sarah Hubbard Harris, who married Denison Lathrop and they had a daughter named Sally Lathrop who married Rev. Thomas Kennan.

THEIR CHILDREN WERE.

33—1. George Kennan, son of Rev. Thomas and Sally (Lathrop) Kennan, born at Waterbury, Vt., Oct. 8, 1795.

34—2. Abigail Kennan, daughter of Rev. Thomas and Sally (Lathrop) Kennan, born May 6, 1797. Died Feb. 2, 1865.

35—3. Clarissa Kennan, daughter of Rev. Thomas and Sally (Lathrop) Kennan, born March 1, 1801. Died March 18, 1831.

36—4. John Kennan, son of Rev. Thomas and Sally (Lathrop) Kennan, born March 7, 1803.

37—5. Philena Kennan, daughter of Rev. Thomas and Sally (Lathrop) Kennan, born March 21, 1805.

38—6. Sarah H. Kennan, daughter of Rev. Thomas and Sally (Lathrop) Kennan, born May 16, 1808.

39—7. Sophronia Kennan, daughter of Rev. Thomas and Sally (Lathrop) Kennan, born July 18, 1811.

40—8. Jairus Kennan, son of Rev. Thomas and Sally (Lathrop) Kennan, born at Moira, N. Y., April 22, 1813.

Names of Persons in the foregoing Picture

1. The gentleman standing at your left hand is John Kennan.

2. The lady standing at the left hand of John Kennan is his wife Mary Ann (Morse) Kennan.

A page from *Genealogy of the Kennan Family* by Thomas L. Kennan, 1907.

THREE

Abigail

n the preceding chapter, concentration was placed on the first generation of the family—on James Kennan and his wife, Margaret, that is, and, in a general sense on their children. But it was of course his second son, George, born in 1752, who was to carry forward the line of inheritance we are pursuing. This being so, it is proposed, in the present chapter, to look more carefully at George's life and, in particular, at the identity of his wife, Abigail, and the circumstances that brought her into the family.

Let us begin by noting that the move of the family from the Holden vicinity to that of Charlemont was accomplished, in stages, in the years from 1769 to 1773. Mention has already been made of some of the circumstances surrounding this move: of Mr. Booth's retirement from the deal; and of the dispatch of father James Kennan and his second son, George, as an advance party to prepare the ground for the reception of the remainder of the family at the Charlemont end of the move. And now, since it is George's life that stands at the forefront of our inquiry, it becomes necessary to have a closer look at the wider background of these events. The reader should be forewarned that the evidence over those crucial years 1769–1773 is, while often suggestive, scanty and, on the face of it, confusing.

For the advance mission of father to Charlemont to prepare for the final move of the family there is ample evidence. The volume of Tax Evaluations of the State of Massachusetts for the year 1771 shows, under the name "James McKannon" [*sic*], as residents in the town of Charlemont, "two adult polls-rateable" males, the owners of fifteen-shillingsworth of real estate, three oxen, and three acres of mowing land, calculated to yield three tons of fresh hay per annum. Confusing as in some respects they are, these figures show clearly that the persons in question were in the process of acquiring and taking over some sort of a farming property. Where they were residing at the time—whether in a main farmhouse or in some sort of smaller structure—is unclear. But that they *were* there, and that in the year 1771, is clear. The reader is asked to hold this in mind as we now turn to the person of Abigail.

My grandfather, when writing his book on the family, confessed his failure to find out anything at all about the wife of the young George Kennan except her name: Abigail Sherman. And I, too, taking up the investigation some seven decades later, found myself at first similarly frustrated. There were, to grandfather's knowledge as to mine, no Shermans in the Holden or Charlemont regions. What, then, was a woman bearing the Sherman name doing, marrying in Charlemont in approximately 1772 our young

George, and doing so in such unusual circumstances as then prevailed?

Learning that there were many Shermans in southern Connecticut, I appealed to the small but excellent historical society in Stratford for help. Some time passed. Information was not readily available. But one day a senior figure in that Society got in touch to tell me that they had just found record of a certain Abigail Sherman, born in 1747 in the town of Woodbury, Connecticut. She was, it appeared, the daughter of one Daniel Sherman and his wife, named Mary. This discovery, for which I was and have remained intensely appreciative, was the departure point for a long, interesting, if often frustrating effort to learn more about the Abigail in question (without doubt my own great-great-great-grandmother).

The first step was inquiry into her parentage. Let me take first her father, Daniel Sherman. He was probably born, I discover, in Stratford or thereabouts. Of his antecedents I could learn very little, other than that his father appears to have been, at least at one time, an Anglican. Daniel's birth probably occurred at some time around 1725–1726. When he was a child or a small boy, his own father died. The mother soon found another husband; and, taking at least some of her children (or most of them) with her, went off to live at her new husband's home. But when Daniel turned fifteen, in the year 1740, he was permitted (or required, I do not know which) to select a guardian of his own. This he did, the choice falling on a somewhat older cousin of his, a certain Job Sherman, resident of the nearby place called Newtown. In this way, Daniel became a resident of that place. But not for long, because the guardianship was brief. At the age of eighteen or shortly thereafter, Daniel became officially an adult, or at least he seems no longer to have needed a guardian. And it was there, then, in Newtown, that he met and married, in 1745, a native and resident of that town, one Mary Northrup.

The name which Newtown enjoyed was a suitable one, for the place had been only recently founded, in the early eighteenth century, by three Northrup brothers, one of whom, Abigail's grandfather, was a man known as Lieutenant John Northrup. Not only had he taken part in the founding of the town, but he served it for some thirty years as selectman and town clerk. Both of these, we might note, were positions that presupposed a reasonably high educational level.

The wife of this John Northrup, Abigail's grandmother, was a Mary Porter. Her own father and grandfather had both been what would today be known as physicians—a term not then in use in New England (those who rendered medical services often combining that activity with other professional pursuits, such as that of barber, and being generally referred to as "bone-setters"). The Porters, plainly, were again highly educated people. And as for Mary Porter herself, she, born in 1698, lived (as was rare in the colonial society of that day) to the age of ninety-seven. She was thus, in the Northrup family, a striking matriarchal figure, carrying on down and through the lives of most of her grandchildren, including our Abigail.

All these circumstances tend to suggest that the Northrup family into which Mary was born was distinctly better educated and more widely experienced than the Sherman family into which she married. There is, after all, nothing to suggest that the Daniel

Sherman she married was anything other than a very ordinary and colorless person, a man whose professional interests were limited to farming, and whose personal character was somewhat short of a reliable stability.

The marriage of Daniel Sherman and Mary Northrup took place in Newtown in 1745. Abigail, as already noted, was born in 1747. She was the first of five children to be born to that couple in the following thirteen years, the last, born in 1760, being a boy. (And this makes her, we might note, some four or five years older than the George Kennan she was to marry.)

But those thirteen years, and a further ten that followed, were ones full of uncertainties and puzzles for the family historian. Where did the family of Daniel Sherman and Mary Northrup live? There seems to be a great confusion in answers. They are often mentioned (to the extent they are mentioned at all) in connection with the neighboring town of Woodbury; and indeed some of Daniel's affairs would suggest that sort of a connection. But here we are again confronted, as we were in tracing earlier movements of the family, with the habit, so widespread in colonial New England, of applying the name "town" not just to the little built-up administrative center of a large surrounding rural area but to the rest of that area as well. So unless one knows the township boundaries, one can seldom be sure what the expression "town" really means. I find no evidence of any actual residence of Daniel's family in Woodbury proper. I do find, however, evidence of its involvement with the smaller "town" of Roxbury, which was situated some six miles distant from inner Woodbury, but was officially included, at that time, in the wider Woodbury township.

After plodding through a depressing number of documents I can now only give it as the most plausible hypothesis that Daniel, soon after the marriage, acquired a small farm in the neighborhood of Roxbury, and that it was there that he and his family lived over the following twenty-some years. But this circumstance, if true, would have been of high importance; for it would imply that Abigail, although descended from the well-educated Northrup family, was brought up as a farm-and-village girl, and not as one long exposed, as I had previously thought to be the case, to the educational and social life of a long-settled and mature community such as Woodbury. And this might also explain why it was that she, up to the time of the family's move to Massachusetts (about to be described) in the late 1760s, had found, in Roxbury or its environs, no inviting possibilities for marriage.

Be that as it may, there is evidence that in the years 1766 to 1768 Daniel Sherman sold off his farmland in Connecticut and moved to the "town" of Adams in northwestern Massachusetts. His presence there as early as 1768 seems to be confirmed. His name appears as that of a resident of "Adams" in the 1790 federal census. But he was, by profession, only a farmer. And was this not then another instance of a town's name being given to large tracts of wholly agricultural country around a rural center?

Evidence available in the Stratford records suggests the Daniel, in moving north into Massachusetts, was accompanied, at least on departure, by two of his daughters—Abigail, the oldest of the children, and a slightly younger sister. (What happened to the remainder of his family—wife and three other children—is nowhere evident.) But between that reasonably documented departure and the appearance of Abigail, only one or two years later, on or at the new farm of the Kennans near Charlemont there lies a gap in the family history for the filling of which there is almost no documentary evidence at all. The family historian is therefore left to find his way in the admittedly imperfect world of surmises—but surmises taking account of such subsidiary information as is, at this point, available.

A portion of the route by which the small Sherman party would normally have made their way from southern Connecticut northward lay along the banks of the Connecticut River. This would have taken them through the town of Windsor, which was a natural stopping-off place for north-south travelers. For the Shermans, in particular, this would have had a special attraction, because it housed one of the two major centers of Booth settlement in the state of Connecticut. And there had been close connections among the Booth family, the Shermans, and the Northrups in Newtown where they had all fairly recently resided. The Northrups and the Booths were related by a recent marriage. And relations between the Booths and the Shermans were even closer. Daniel Sherman had in fact bought, together with a certain David Booth, of Newtown, the farmland near Roxbury where he was to farm for so many years. And here now was James Kennan, doing twenty years later something very similar, though with another Booth and in a different place.

Now, the most likely date we can find for the move of Abigail's father to Adams would have been 1768 or 1769. And this, too, seems the most likely time for the agreement between Aaron Booth and James Kennan for joint purchase of the Charlemont farm. Not only that, but Daniel Sherman's route to Adams would with high probability have taken him through both Windsor and Charlemont. This being so, it is not at all impossible that the two parties, Aaron Booth and the three Shermans, met in Windsor and traveled together as far as Charlemont, and that Booth suggested that Abigail, now a mature woman of some 21 years of age, be dropped off there to serve as the same sort of advance party as the Kennans then constituted, but now for the purpose of preparing things for the anticipated early arrival of the remainder of the Booth family.

We must note, in this connection, that the joint purchase of the farm that Booth and Kennan were then contemplating would have plainly assumed the availability on the Charlemont property of two residential buildings. It would have been quite out of the question that the two families, with their numerous children, could have been planning to occupy a single home. This, in turn, suggests that the purchase the two men had in mind was not of a single farm but of two adjacent ones, each provided with a farmer's residence. Nothing else would have made sense. How appropriate, then, that Abigail should be asked to drop off in Charlemont to make one of the residences suitable for the arrival of the Booth family. It is not only possible but quite probable that the state in which these structures had been abandoned by their former owners required a good deal of setting to rights before another family was poured into either of them.

Now this surmise would have placed Abigail in one of those two places at almost exactly the time that the two Kennans, father and son, arrived on the scene and busied themselves with preparing the other place for occupancy. And we may place the time when all this happened at something like 1769 or, at the latest, 1770.

The arrival of the remainder of the Kennan family, let us remember, was not expected before about 1773. There was ample time, then, for the two advance parties to become well acquainted before the crucial year of 1772. I say "crucial" because it is in this year, 1772, that such documentary evidence as exists confirms the marriage of George Kennan (now twenty years old) and Abigail Sherman (by about four years his senior). This evidence comes from the incredibly rich biographical archives of the great Family History Library in Salt Lake City, Utah. Here a single page names 1772 as indeed the date of the marriage, *but* names the place of it as Rutland, whence the Kennans were now moving. This, in turn, suggests that George went to the trouble of taking his intended bride back to the place where his parents, although probably already preparing for the move to Charlemont, were still holding forth. This had important advantages. It made possible marriage in the church where George's father had a pew, and it also made it possible for Abigail to become acquainted in a proper manner with her future mother-in-law and to obtain the latter's consent to the marriage, which, in the circumstances, was of highest importance.

All this, then, was apparently accomplished. It must, however, have put an end to George's usefulness in any further preparation for the arrival of the family at the Charlemont end. The return to Rutland and the conduct of the marriage would have preempted, at a minimum, the three years 1771 through 1773; and one can only conclude that he returned to Charlemont, together with the remainder of the family, in the last of those years.

By January 1773, in any case, Abigail's pregnancy, it appears, became evident. And the child, a boy, was born in early June. Given the name Thomas, he was destined to be, some years down the line, the last patriarch of the last of these three first generations of the American family.

It will be well to note that this marriage, from the parents' standpoint, was not without its advantages. The departure and disappearance of Aaron Booth must have left the Kennans with two houses on new property they were taking over. And this served more than one purpose. For it was a firm and long-standing rule of New England society that when a son married, he must never try to take his bride and progeny back into his parents' home for regular residence. He and his bride must find a home of their own. This necessity was met beautifully, in the case at hand, by the existence of the second house on the property. And since the abundant James Kennan family would have crowded even the best of farmhouses in that period, the availability of a second farmhouse not only provided a place where George and Abigail could establish their household but also relieved the Kennan parents of at least one of the sons in their own crowded household.

One may wonder to what extent the rather sudden marriage of George and Abigail was a response to the urgings of young love, or to what extent it was viewed by the parties as a *mariage de convenance.*

The writer hopes that it will not be regarded as too

speculative if he points out that there may have been elements of both motivations in the minds of both parties, but that as between the two, the consideration of *convenance* probably prevailed more strongly in Abigail's case than in the other. For a girl of a simple country family of that time to reach the age of twenty-four and be still unmarried was to find herself in a precarious situation. Professional positions open to such a person, restricted in many cases to school-teaching, tended to be few and very poorly paid. There were practically no prospects other than marriage for escape from the parental household and for avoiding the slide into the unhappy status of old maid. Most girls were well aware of this reality; and Abigail, too, must have had it clearly in mind.

However that may be, the marriage lasted—lasted, in fact, for some fifty further years, into both their old ages. And it produced a crop of ten children, all born during this Charlemont period. Four of these died in infancy or early childhood, which was about par for the course at that time. But the others lived and apparently prospered; and we shall have opportunity to pursue some of their lives further in the following chapters of this account.

The Charlemont period in the family's life was to extend over two decades. What George did, professionally, over all this time is only in small part visible. The father, as we have already noted, died sometime around the year 1780, some seven years after the family's arrival. We may suppose that George, presumably living on the farm, threw himself, together with the father, into the operation of the enterprise so long as the father was alive. After his death, the farm, or much of it, seems to have been taken out of operation and various parts of it bequeathed to the various brothers and the widow, who then sold them off at their convenience. Whether this included the two residences we have no means of knowing. The children of George and Abigail must have attended the Charlemont schools, although of this, too, we have no confirmed evidence. (Massachusetts law made compulsory for every sizable community the maintenance of proper instruction at the elementary level.) And of George himself we have little information, beyond the fact that after the father's death he took an active part in the local-government affairs of the Charlemont community, serving at various times as a member of the Committee of Public Safety, as selectman (i.e., a member of the town's municipal council), and as assessor and highway surveyor. He was even entrusted at one time with the distribution of the "school money"—a responsibility which made particular demands on public confidence. But such remuneration as he might have received for these services would have been far from sufficient for the maintenance of his growing family. He had had no occupational experience other than as a farmer. And there is no evidence that he acquired, or even wanted to acquire, another farm in place of the one that was being broken up, especially since he would presumably have been wholly alone in the operation of it. The father, in farming in the Charlemont region, had presumably had at least George's help. But in any further farming activities George would have been alone.

In this connection it may be well, at this point, to take account of the heavily strained relationships of George with his four brothers. We have already noted that all four of the latter marched to the colors in the

Revolutionary War. Their names, ranks, periods of service and assignments, together with identification of the units in which they served, are all faithfully recorded in the great series entitled *Massachusetts Soldiers and Sailors in the Revolutionary War*, published in 1902. The only brother whose name does not thus appear is George. There is no evidence that he ever performed such a service.

What, then, was this historian's bewilderment upon finding George figuring in the town records for 1782, only some four years after the completion of the military services of his brothers, as "Lieutenant" and continuing to bear that title over the remaining years of his residence in Charlemont. He was also listed as "Ltn." in the first, 1790, census of the United States. If this title had not been earned by service in the war (and there is no evidence that it had been), one can imagine with what hoots of derision the appearance of it must have been greeted by his brothers, all of whom had so served and none of whom had received an officer's commission.

To make matters worse, we have the fact that in the deeds providing for the disposal of what were evidently the lands of the farm, shortly after father James's death, George seems to have been consistently referred to as "George Kennan, Gentleman" whereas, in contrast, one of his younger brothers is designated on a similar deed as "Isaac Kennan, Yeoman." How to explain?

Actually, one can think of reasons less than wholly discreditable for both of these apparent anomalies. Of the five brothers, George was the only one, or so it would appear, who, at the time of the outbreak of the Revolutionary War, was married and the father of small children, whom, together with their mother, he was obliged to support. (Actually, one of these children was being born precisely on the day of the first call to the colors of at least one of the brothers in connection with the Bunker Hill action.) Then there was, too, presumably the farm, where his presence may well have been plainly required. And as far as the title "Lieutenant" was concerned, it would appear that such positions were not at that time normally earned by previous service in the ranks but were, following the late British custom, conferred by the governor for various reasons, not all of which necessarily had anything to do with military experience or competence.

And finally, as for the designation of our George in official deeds as "Gentleman," in contrast to his brother's title of "Yeoman," it seems clear that such designations varied primarily with the amount of tillable land the subject could be shown to possess, and whether that land was worked entirely by hired or indentured labor or whether the owner contributed some of the work himself. In all of this, our George's situation might well have justified the description.

But recognizing the peculiar sensibilities that so often attend the competitive interrelationships of brothers, one may suspect that even if those honorific distinctions that came to rest on George were ones conferred purely by circumstances, it was with something less than fraternal understanding that the brothers took note of them.

George's appointments and associated activities raise the question: Where, during precisely those years of the early 1780s, did he and his family reside? We have assumed that they resided, up to this point, somewhere in the vicinity of East Charlemont, where George could be readily at hand to help with the operation of the farm. But it would have been wholly impractical for him to exercise these various local offices at such a distance from the Charlemont center. He must surely, in these circumstances, have sought and occupied a residence more conveniently located for the carrying out of these responsibilities.

And here, we might note, another curious set of circumstances enters in. In the years from 1773 to 1779, when family life centered around the father's farm and George and his own family presumably lived in that vicinity, 3 children, all sons, were born to George and his wife, Abigail. All three survived the vicissitudes of early childhood and grew rapidly to manhood. From the year of the father's death, however, and of the presumed move of the family to some place nearer the Charlemont center, in some five years thereafter, another 5 children were born, and of these, 4 were carried off, in early childhood, by disease. Does this not suggest that the place to which they had moved was in some way seriously unhealthy? After the mid-1780s, at a time when there is no evidence of further occupancy by George of these various local offices, the situation changed again. Two more children were born in the succeeding years of the 1780s, and these appear to have thrived and lived on to maturity. So another question poses itself. Were those years of special prominence for George in local public affairs (approximately 1780 to 1785) not ones of much sadness and unhappiness for his wife?

The final years of the 1780s constitute one of those gaps in the available record, so total, so unrelenting, that even the imagination of the historian quails at the penetration of them. George's services to the Charlemont community seem, for some unimaginable reason, to have petered out long before the end of the decade. We find ourselves hoping that he and his family found a healthier place to live in Charlemont. But even that sort of remission does not make a life; and in any case, we do not know.

It is perhaps permissible to doubt that Abigail ever fully accepted life in Charlemont after her personal disasters of the early part of that particular decade. Of George and his doings we simply know nothing at all. We are confronted only with the stark fact that the last year of the 1780s seems to have found the family (now including one or two boys old enough at least to raise a voice in the family deliberations) contemplating a complete removal from the Charlemont region to a place in central Vermont called Waterbury. Abigail had at least a nephew who had recently founded an existence there; and his encouragement must have taken a prominent place in the family's decision.

This encouragement was certainly an important factor in the decision of the Kennans to make this move. But the decision, on the face of it, was a strange one. What then bore the name of Waterbury (for the very few people who had ever heard of it) offered no amenities for civilized living comparable to those the Kennans were presumably about to give up in Charlemont; and of this they must have been aware. Yet they seem to have accepted with alacrity the nephew's encouragement of the move. And there is no evidence that Charlemont, as they had known and experienced it, posed any serious counter-considerations.

Indeed, the relationship of the George Kennan family to Charlemont is generally a puzzling one. Two decades of life in a single community does not pass for any family, particularly any with growing children, without the growth of some bonds of association and acquaintance, if not friendship, with other members of the community in question. In the case at hand, all of the Kennan children must, one supposes, have attended the local schools. The father, at one time, had served in a number of modest local offices. Yet there is not the slightest evidence that any of these associations stood in the way of the rather startling decision to move, at the end of the 1790s, to a remote and uncertain destination.

And the break with Charlemont seems to have been a clean and lasting one. One hears of no return visit by any member of the family—ever—to that community. None of the children seem, upon reaching maturity, ever to have revisited the place. The move once accomplished, the very name "Charlemont" seems to have dropped out of the family's vocabulary.

And vice versa. If the family forgot Charlemont, that place, with no less finality, forgot them. I find no mention of any Kennan in any of its histories. Small wonder that my wife and I, on our brief visit to that place in 1968, had no response to our various inquiries other than one of complete bewilderment.

How to explain the totality of this break? Imagination, as usual, comes up with suggestions, but none with any solid plausibility. There is, however, one small matter that ought, perhaps, to be mentioned in this connection.

In posing the question (see Chapter II, above) of what might have moved the first generation of those Kennans to choose the Charlemont vicinity over any others, as their first and presumably final destination for the first move, I noted that they might have been influenced by contacts with the small Scottish community—a rather compact village of Scots, in fact—situated not far from Charlemont. It now becomes necessary to give that community a little greater attention.

This was initially a purely Ulster-Scottish settlement, given the name of Colrain, and positioned, as I make it, some ten to twelve miles northeast of Charlemont. It was formally set up, by permission of the colonial authorities, in 1741, just three years before the marriage of James and Margaret Kennan.

I should perhaps have mentioned at an earlier point in this disquisition that the Bostonian authorities, in politely ushering to the adjacent interior (then largely known as Worcester) the hundreds of passengers from the flotilla of ships from northern Ireland that arrived at the port of Boston in the period 1718–1721, were motivated by two considerations. The first was to keep these immigrants out of Boston, where they were not wanted and for the relatively urban life of which they were indeed poorly prepared. But the second consideration was the desire to build up population in that region just west of Boston as a means of repelling, and keeping at a distance, the Indians, who, in those years, were still making occasional trouble there.

Few of these Scottish immigrants would appear to have formed compact settlements in the new environment. The establishment of family farms alone tended to disperse them; and most of them merged as best they could, as isolated families, into the surrounding countryside. The compact little settlement called Colrain was thus a rare exception. And the number of its inhabitants was sufficient to permit purely Scottish marriages, comparable to that of James and Margaret Kennan. The atmosphere of the place must thus have been that of an unadulterated Scottishness. The Kennans must have been at all times keenly aware of the existence and national character of the place.

Only recently, just as this chapter on Charlemont was under completion, did the writer of these lines stumble on a document—a page from the printed results of the first United States census—which opened new vistas, or potential vistas, for the final years of the Kennans' residence in the Charlemont region. It was a page on which were recorded the census findings for the village of Colrain. And here, on a listing of the households of the village, the writer was startled to discover the name of none other than Lieutenant George Kennan.

At first glance, the writer's reaction was only one of bewilderment, and he was inclined to give this only the briefest mention in his account. But further contemplation brought him to the realization that it might actually have been here, in this Colrain house, that the Kennans were living in the final years of the 1780s and the first of the 1790s, prior to the move to Vermont.

The reasons that speak for the plausibility of this suggestion are too numerous to be listed here. But two of them stand out. One is the recognition that George Kennan is unlikely to have owned, at that time, two houses, one in Charlemont and one in Colrain, and that of the two the only one proven to exist (in this case, by the census figures) was the one most likely to have been the actual residence. The other reason for the suggestion of such a residence is that this would provide the only conceivable explanation for the total and otherwise inexplicable dearth of any evidence of the presence, must less the doings, of the Kennan family in the town of Charlemont over these years. In the absence of any such evidence, the years in question, as mentioned above, constituted a complete blank, a "black hole," so to speak, in the family's history. The suggestion of a residence in Colrain, implying as it does that they were not then living in Charlemont at all, provides the first potential breach in that wall of ignorance.

Should there be any reality behind this suggestion, the question would at once present itself: what was the nature of the family's life in this new environment? It would be the first time they had ever lived in so small, tight, and well-established a community, and particularly in one founded on so strict a sense of national identity. For the father, George, himself a full-blooded Scot, this would have presented fewer problems. But for Abigail things would have been more complicated. She was not a Scot. She was of the purest English-colonial, southern-Connecticut origins, and was the child of a family much better educated than would have been the case with most of the wives in this Scottish frontier settlement. It is not easy to picture her being readily and warmly accepted in the latter's company.

But this is all still speculative, and should not be allowed to carry us too far. There is no reason to suppose that a few years' residence in Colrain would ever have been viewed by either George or Abigail as anything other than an interim solution to the problem of finding a secure and permanent home to replace the one-time farmhouse that they had now abandoned.

It is also clear that in the last of the years the family could conceivably have spent in Colrain, Abigail's hopes and calculations were turning to other possible solutions to the problem just mentioned, a subject that leads us directly to the next chapter of this account.

Gravestone of George Kennan (1752–1830)
in Waterbury, Vermont, cemetery.

FOUR

Waterbury

he expanse of territory now known as Vermont was, up to the time of the American Revolution and even thereafter until it was accepted as a state of the Union in 1791, a species of political and institutional no-man's-land. It was covered largely by undeveloped forest. It was not a British colony, nor was it the colony of any other power. New Hampshire and New York and occasionally even Quebec claimed control over parts of it. And there was a furious competition, among public authorities and private parties of all these surrounding regions, in the advancement of claims of possession of Vermont lands. Claims in the name of public authority (of the governor of New Hampshire, for example) were sometimes immense. The private claims, however, appear to have been limited to six-mile-side (thirty-six-square-mile) squares. In many instances, and particularly as concerned those parts of the territory in which we are interested, the claims were advanced not only by individuals but more often by groups of relatively affluent speculators.

Most of these latter had no idea of settling personally on their claimed plots, but they anticipated the eventual development of the land in question, and, having paid little or nothing for it in the first instance, they looked forward to handsome future profits by sale to those who would eventually settle on it.

One of these groups of claimants was composed mostly of some prosperous gentlemen from Connecticut and New Jersey. Their charter, issued by the governor of New Hampshire (who then claimed sovereignty over this entire territory), was formally granted as early as 1763; but for nearly twenty years thereafter, the plot to which they laid claim remained virtually untouched, only a theoretically designated space, still surrounded by the forests which at that time still covered so much of that portion of Vermont. The 1763 charter described the area in question as Waterbury, taking the name presumably from the Connecticut town of that name.

Why this tract rather than any other was chosen I have never learned. Probably because a forest foot trail traversing the region between the Connecticut River and Lake Champlain led through it. However that may have been, the remote proprietors, probably sensing imminent development and wishing to formalize their claim, sent, in 1782, a surveying party to mark off their plot, presumably by stakes at the comers of the square. To shelter themselves during the several days of their work, the surveyors erected a small shack, which they left in place upon their departure. Otherwise the plot was left in its original peaceful condition in the forest.

The following year, however, in early spring, there arrived, on snowshoes, the first prospective settler, a strong and experienced frontiersman by the name of James Marsh. (He appears, incidentally, to have been a man marked out by fate for undeserved but regular misfortunes.) He had come, in this instance, alone, leaving his family—wife and eight children—in a settlement some twenty miles distant. He apparently spent much of the summer living in the surveyor's shack, clearing some land, growing a crop of corn, and preparing for the arrival of the entire family in the following season. He then returned, to spend the winter with the rest of them.

In the following spring, in 1784, he formed a small advance party to prepare the place for the arrival of the family. This party consisted of himself, three young children (all on snowshoes and pulling a sled), and a dog. To his consternation, he found most of his corn supply had disappeared (cause unknown). Realizing that some new supply of food would have to be provided to take its place, and this before the rest of the family could be brought on, he decided to return at once to make the arrangements. Installing the three children (a boy of fifteen, a girl of twelve, and another male person described by historians only as "a small boy") in the shack, and supplying them with what he thought would be enough fish and game to hold them for a week, he then returned to fetch the remainder of the family. But here, unexpected difficulties were encountered; three weeks passed rather than a single one. Frantic with anxiety for the children, he bundled up the rest of the family and made the final move with them, only to find the place deserted and the ashes of the fire in the shack completely cold. And here was he, now, with eight people on his hands, and all largely dependent for food on such fish and game as he could extract from the small stream that flowed through the place and from the surrounding woods.

He had heard of another settlement, some thirteen miles away. To this he sent another boy, who made it successfully through the forest and returned some days later with the missing children. They, it seems, after consuming their week's rations, had lived another week on the roots of wild onions; and then, in the third week, sensibly recognizing that in another two or three days they would be emaciated even beyond the possibility of walking, they set out in the direction of a reputed other settlement. Rather miraculously (probably with the help of the dog, who saved them en route by driving away an enormous bear), they found the settlement, were received with kindness and concern by the people living there, and, after spending some days recovering sufficiently to eat solid food, they rejoined the family. Through what further hardships I shudder to think, the family then stuck it out, built their cabin, and remained to do their part in the ultimate development of the town called Waterbury. It remains only to be noted that the unhappy Marsh father, in 1785, on the very day of arrival of a second family coming to settle there, fell victim to his own joy and excitement over this event and, trying to make a hurried passage over the still partly frozen river, fell in and drowned.

Why do I tell all this? I do it for what it says, or fails to say, about that generation of the Kennan family we have been considering. We have spoken, albeit without much success, of the reasons that might have inclined them to leave Charlemont—the place *from which* they were departing. And now we have to ask ourselves: what, in their eyes, were the charms of the place *to which* they were now deciding to go?

What, at the time of the move, 1793, did the family consist of? Of the original ten children, four are definitely known to have died in childhood. Of the remaining six, only three, all of them boys, can be plainly shown to have accompanied the family to Vermont. Of the other three, all girls, nothing is known. Of the three boys who did come along, the oldest—Thomas, about twenty—had presumably exhausted all such educational benefits as Charlemont had to offer. The next in line, George Jr., was sixteen. Perhaps whatever he had learned in Charlemont schools was considered to suffice. But the youngest and brightest, Jairus, was only about ten. And there was at that time no school in Waterbury. What, one wonders, did they expect to do about him?

The most immediate encouragement for the move plainly came from a nephew of Abigail's, one Stiles Sherman, who, with wife and small but growing family, had become the fourth settler in Waterbury, arriving in 1788. He had built his own log house there; and there he was to remain, as a prominent citizen, for the rest of his life. There must indeed have been some strange attraction to the small valley where Waterbury is situated, for so many of those who came to it in the initial pioneer days chose to spend the rest of their lives there. But how Stiles Sherman depicted the charms of the place in encouraging the Kennans to move there we do not know. It was, after all, at that time still a very primitive little forest enclosure. It must have been rosy visions of the future that took the leading place in Stiles Sherman's optimistic urgings.

And perhaps they were not entirely misplaced. For the population, consisting of only three families when Stiles Sherman moved there, had grown, by the time the Kennans arrived in 1793, to the number of some fifteen families, embracing ninety-three people. And the little community was destined to grow even more rapidly in the years that followed.

Still, the decision to make the move was, in the light of all that we know, a curious one; and we are reduced to the conclusion that of the two possible motives behind it—the dissatisfaction with life in Charlemont or the depicted beauties of life in Waterbury—it was the former rather than the latter that played the determining part.

Upon arrival in Waterbury in 1793, the first thing the Kennan family must have done was to construct its own house; and this structure, situated beside that of Abigail's nephew, must have been fairly commodious, for it was used, at least for some years, as an inn, accommodating primarily people in transit from the Connecticut River settlements to the ones on Lake Champlain. And we might wish to note that the position of father George Kennan as an innkeeper was the first identifiable instance, on the part of anyone in that branch of the family, of any regular occupation other than that of farmer.

To understand how the Kennans related to the Waterbury community a few words will be in order about the condition of that place in 1793. It was then two years since Vermont had been admitted as a state of the Union, the first territory to gain that status which had not been one of the original colonies. But even before Vermont achieved statehood, the tiny

Waterbury community had set up its own democratic life. And leadership in this process had been exercised by a most remarkable man, the dominant personality in the community, by the name of Ezra Butler. He had been, in 1788, the first permanent settler, and was destined not only to play for many years the leading role in developing the community but also to retain his residence there throughout the remainder of his life.

He had risen from the most humble of backgrounds: the son of a poor family broken by the early death of the mother, at a time when he himself was very young. After receiving no more than a grade-school education, he was consigned for some years, as an indentured servant, to a doctor in eastern Vermont. After completing that service, he came in 1785, in company with his brother, Asaph, and for reasons I have never ascertained, on a preliminary visit, likewise on snowshoes, to Waterbury. The following year, having in the meantime married, and being now still only twenty-two years of age, he made a permanent move to Waterbury, together with his young wife, and built his own log house for shelter. When Butler had made his first exploratory visit, in 1785, James Marsh was still there; but when he came there for good, Marsh had died, in consequence of which he, Butler, came to be regarded not only as the first settler but as the patriarch of the community that was about to be developed.

Ezra Butler was, at the time of his move to Waterbury, wholly irreligious. He was, however, deeply affected, shortly after his move there, by a pamphlet left in the place by an itinerant Baptist revivalist who had evidently passed through the settlement at an earlier date. The result was that he was converted for life, and several years later was even formally ordained as a Baptist minister.

Modest and quiet to a point in his behavior, Butler was a man of unquestionable personal honesty and integrity and of unbending firmness in matters of principle. To complete the picture of him, I must reach ahead to mention that in later years he was to enter into public affairs on a much wider scale, becoming a member of Vermont's state legislature, a presiding judge of its supreme court, the state's representative in the national Congress, and eventually (1826) the governor of the state of Vermont. All these offices he held without abandoning his residence and interests in Waterbury.

Given his position of leadership in that community, Butler was of course well known to the Kennan boys, and they to him. It is safe to say that they had never known anyone of Butler's qualities in eastern Massachusetts or in Charlemont. And he must have been what today would be called a "role model" for all three of them.

Father George Kennan, having had extensive experience in local public affairs in Charlemont, immediately upon his arrival in Waterbury assumed his share of such duties in the Waterbury community. Only a year after arrival, he was already serving as moderator and selectman, and he held for many years a position as justice of the peace. In two instances in the years from 1798 to 1815, he served, by election, in the Vermont legislature, relieving in those years Ezra Butler, who was normally the occupant of that position but was sometimes obliged to give it up temporarily in order to meet the demands of his several other public offices.

Of the three sons who accompanied the family from Charlemont to Waterbury, George, named after his father and now approximately sixteen years old, seems to have been the only one who married and settled permanently in Waterbury. He was recognized throughout as a respectable member of the community, occupying the positions of constable in 1802 and selectman in 1809.

Thomas, the oldest of the sons, the one who had been born in 1773 in or around Charlemont in the curious circumstances recounted above, was now by the time of the arrival of the family in Waterbury a young man twenty years of age. Because it was he who was the forefather of the later generations of the family with which this treatise is concerned, he has to be given a special place in this account. Most of what has to be said about him will have to be reserved for later chapters, dealing with the circumstances of his mature professional and personal life. But because his permanent career, which was to be that of minister of the gospel, and his early development as a husband and father could well be said to have begun in Waterbury, a few words about what occurred to him during those first years of the Waterbury period will not be out of order.

We have first of all to note that not long after his arrival in Waterbury he married and became the first father of another generation. His bride was a certain Sally Lathrop. There was no Lathrop family in the Waterbury community, and we are obliged to conclude that he must have met Sally during the passage of the family on its way to Waterbury, through the town in eastern Vermont where she had grown up, and that some sort of engagement must then have been concluded; for the two were married on February 19, 1795, by none other than Ezra Butler, functioning here as justice of the peace.

The Lathrop family in which Sally had grown up, like all the other families into which the Kennans of that time either had married or were about to marry, was one that traced its American roots to people who came from England either on or shortly after the *Mayflower*. By the later part of the eighteenth century, the Lathrop family had multiplied greatly, and various of its branches had produced, in their time, persons of much distinction. Of the immediate family of our Sally this could not be said; but there is no reason to doubt that they were a respectable family, who had followed the common movement of such people from Connecticut (in this case, New London) northward to Vermont. That Sally made a fine wife for Thomas Kennan was to be amply demonstrated in the years that lay ahead.

After their marriage in February 1795, Thomas and Sally lost no time in producing the first of their several children. This was a boy named George, born in October of that same year, and destined to become the great-grandfather of him who writes these lines. After that, several other children were produced at the usual intervals, some being born in Waterbury, others in the places to which, only a few years later, the father and mother moved.

The quality in the life of this Thomas Kennan that distinguished him from other male Kennans, both before his time and after it, was an active religious commitment. This became evident almost immediately in the Waterbury years. Where it had its origins, we do not know—very possibly with the example of Ezra Butler. It was, in any case, a commitment that would carry him into his life's work as a minister of the gospel in several Presbyterian communities.

How this commitment could have been aroused and developed in the Waterbury of the late 1790s is an interesting question. It certainly could not have had much encouragement from Thomas's own family, which had shown little if any interest in religious matters in the Charlemont period. That Ezra Butler served as the strong example of the firm Christian believer is probable; but he, being a Baptist, is unlikely to have been a teacher for the young Kennan, for the commitment of the latter appears to have been, from the outset, a firmly Presbyterian-Congregationalist one. A more likely source of encouragement may have been the appearance in Waterbury in 1796 of two gentlemen, one a Deacon Asaph Allen, the other a Mr. Austin, both of them firm believers, Presbyterians apparently, who were shocked to discover upon their arrival that the place harbored no organized religious activity at all and who at once set about organizing Sunday prayer meetings among those who shared their commitment.

But an even more important and likely source of influence on Thomas's development as a religious person was an early Waterbury pioneer by the name of Jonathan Honey. Like so many others of the Waterbury community, he was a native of Connecticut, where he had been trained, and was for a time active, as a lawyer. He appears to have lived in Waterbury, although not yet in any religious capacity, in the late 1790s. He was excellently educated, and a firm Presbyterian. He appears to have served as a teacher for Thomas Kennan's younger brother, Jairus, to whose career we shall turn shortly. Later, in 1802 or 1803, he was ordained and invited to serve as minister of Waterbury's first Congregationalist church, a position he occupied only for some four years, the congregation and the community obviously being, by that time, fed up with him.

For this final reaction there was good reason. For Honey seems to have been of a highly irascible nature and had difficulty getting on with everybody. For years on end he conducted a furious dispute with Ezra Butler over the land on which the latter's house was situated. In the delicate words of one Waterbury historian, the Rev. C. C. Parker, Honey "possessed a clear strong mind, more remarkable for sternness and rigor than for benignity and affability—had more power to convince than to win—to gain respect than affection." All true, no doubt, and unfortunate, if you will. But not necessarily condemnatory for his qualities as a teacher. In pedagogy, too (if I am not mistaken), one can use, depending on circumstances, all kinds of temperaments.

While Thomas Kennan's elementary education was, by the time of the family's move to Waterbury, long in the past, that was not true of his training for service in the church; and it is not unlikely that he had, during his Waterbury years, advanced perceptibly in his preparation for such service. For when, in 1801, a formal large-scale meeting was held to establish Waterbury's first Congregational church, Kennan served, by invitation surely, as secretary to the gathering; and it was not long after that he was himself first baptized and then, shortly thereafter, ordained as a minister.

I must turn now to Jairus, the youngest of the three sons who accompanied the parents on the move from Charlemont to Waterbury. I do this with reluctance and misgiving, for what little we know about him strongly suggests that of all the members of these first three generations of the American branch of the Kennan family, Jairus was the most remarkable and impressive person, yet nowhere are the pockets of obscurity littering our knowledge of the Kennan lives more impenetrable and tantalizing than in his case.

Jairus was born in Charlemont in 1783. He was thus just ten years old when the move to Waterbury occurred, and twelve, let us say, in 1795, when the building of the new home was completed, and when it probably became possible to give serious attention to the problem of his further education.

Now the Waterbury of that time had no school. Such elementary instruction as was available there in the late 1790s was provided, it would seem, by the two young daughters of another citizen of the town, a man by the name of Wells. What they taught must have fallen into the category of what we would call "beginning first grade." And the two sisters were themselves so small in stature, we are told, that they were often confused with their pupils. Instruction at that level was, in any case, not what young Jairus, having surely attended some sort of a school in Charlemont before coming there, now needed.

Yet we find this same Jairus only seven years later entering the first class, consisting of four students, at the fledgling University of Vermont (which graduated him in 1804). But where, in those intervening seven years, had he studied? Where had he been taught?

Here, once again, no answers. There is some evidence that he was tutored in at least a portion of that intervening time by the formidable Jonathan Honey. If so, he would probably have made an adaptable pupil, perhaps even enduring Dr. Honey's severe discipline for the sheer delight of the knowledge imparted. Jairus, to be sure, probably also enjoyed the encouragement and support of Ezra Butler, who, although not at that time a trustee of the new state university, was soon to become one. Still, the seven-year transition from the status of a very young boy in the primitive Waterbury settlement to that of an entering freshman at a university was a remarkable one.

And what happened in the life of young Jairus in the years immediately following his graduation from the university is again a blank spot. Education—and in this case advanced education—must have proceeded in one way or another. But, again, where and what?

An inquiry into the origins and early years of the University of Vermont can well begin with citation of the first sentence of the introductory article by P. Jeffrey Potash in a volume devoted to the history of that institution: "The simultaneous opening of the University of Vermont and of Middlebury College in the fall of 1800," writes Mr. Potash, "was an unprecedented event in the history of New England, where only six colleges and universities had been chartered during the preceding century and a half."*

*Robert V. Daniels, ed., *The University of Vermont: The First Two Hundred Years.* (Hanover, N.H., and London: University Press of New England, 1991).

Actually, the development of both those institutions, at that time the first and only places of higher learning in the state of Vermont, took place very much in the shadow of a bitter rivalry and ill will that marked their mutual relations. Both institutions had their financial problems, but Middlebury was for long in most respects the stronger of the two in academic development, and its foremost personalities fervently yearned to edge the university out of the position of leading academic center of the state, as its name would have implied. And this rivalry between the two institutions was greatly intensified by religious differences. The so-called Great Awakening was now coming to dominate the religious life of large parts of New England, dividing the Congregationalist-Presbyterian clergy between, on the one hand, the conservative and strictly Calvinist school of what could be called "old believers" and, on the other hand, the more modem school of those who, at least by implication, rejected the severe extremisms of Calvinist thought and laid greater weight on purely secular education, as something to be pursued alongside religious studies but not to be wholly dominated by them. This difference marked, at that time, not only the relations between the two relatively new and minor Vermont institutions of higher learning but also those between Harvard and Yale. The latter, under the powerful hand of its highly conservative president, Timothy Dwight, leaned strongly to the orthodox Calvinist side, whereas at Harvard, liberal Unitarianist outlooks predominated. Middlebury College, with the strong support of Timothy Dwight, was dominated by the orthodox Calvinist outlook, whereas the University of Vermont, presided over at the turn of the century and for some years thereafter by the relatively liberal president David Sanders, a Harvard graduate, took the other line. A reader of our present age would find it hard to imagine the intensity of the emotions, and even the hatreds, these differences engendered.

It should also be noted that both of these competing institutions, Middlebury College and the University of Vermont, were, by modern standards, new, poor, and physically primitive entities. When Sanders, in 1814, was finally driven out of office by his ideological opponents, he left the treasury of the university in the possession of exactly $101.06, and with $11,000 in debts. Beyond that the campus suffered grievously from the War of 1812, the town of Burlington, its seat, being shelled by the British navy from the waters of Lake Champlain, and the university's main building being shortly thereafter commandeered and used as a barracks by the American army, causing the complete suspension of all educational activities for several months.

But the university, as a chartered institution, heroically survived these vicissitudes; and it is in that connection that we pick up, once again, credible traces of our Jairus Kennan. At some time in the intervening years, he seems to have been ordained as a minister, presumably in the Congregational Church, although there is no evidence that he ever served actively in that capacity And it is clear that he must, in those years, have pursued higher studies somewhere, presumably in Burlington, the seat of the new university, because by 1813 he was already lecturing at the university, although not yet as a professor.

Then, however, in the years 1813 to 1815, events in his life, and in that of the university, began to tumble over one another in great profusion and confusion. At the end of the institution's fall term of 1813, Kennan left, it appears, for New York City, where, by all evidence, he looked around for a faculty position at one of that city's centers of theological training. But in March of the following year, when the army took over the university buildings and regular pedagogical functions were suspended, there was one branch of academic activity that did not close down; and that was a result of an intense effort of one of the university's trustees, a man by the name of John Pomeroy, a doctor and authority in the field of medicine, to create, in what turned out to be an uneasy association with the university, a medical school. The locus of this enterprise being outside the main university building, it was not affected by the army's takeover of the place. Premises were provided personally by Pomeroy, and the school carried on through the suspension of the university's normal functions, and indeed had a number of students. Pomeroy was anxious to recruit a competent faculty for this institution, and, Kennan having been, it would seem, his first choice for a professorial position, he wrote to Kennan, then still in New York, begging him to return at once and to assume it, it being understood, of course, that the professorship would have to be nominally a university one.

Kennan at first demurred. "I never dreamed," he wrote, "of having a regiment of soldiers to oppose" (the army being still in occupation of the main university building). And if he accepted, he would feel "very much like a professor in a dead college." But he then relented, returned, and joined Pomeroy for teaching in the fall term. And this must have continued, one would think, into the first term of 1815; for on

April 18, the army gave up the university building, and on October 23 of that year Kennan was one of three candidates for professorial appointments (his to be in the fields of chemistry and mineralogy) at the university. But before he could even enter upon his duties as a professor, tragedy struck. He became seriously ill with a tuberculosis, and on January 17, 1816, he died.

Where his death occurred (presumably in Burlington) and who was with him at the end (perhaps his mother; Waterbury was only some forty miles distant) we do not know.

But as a small gloss on those final months of Jairus's life, we might note that here, too, religion played a part. It was only natural that the Great Awakening, strongly orthodox conservative in its enthusiasms, should find the warmest sort of reception at Middlebury; but it was also not without effects on the university's board of trustees. The result was that in 1814, while the active functioning of the university was in abeyance, the relatively liberal Sanders was dropped from its presidency. And when it reopened, in 1815, not only had he been replaced by a more conservative figure, but one of the reasons for the approval by the trustees of the three new professorial appointments, of which Kennan's was one, was that all three were considered to be "of marked religious character," and their appointment was expected to correct what the trustees viewed as an excessive liberalism in the faculty.

To what extent this expectation was justified in the case of Jairus we will never know. To me it does not seem plausible that he could have leaned very strongly to the orthodox side. One may suppose that his status as an ordained minister sufficed, in the eyes of the trustees, to place him in the desired category.

With that, however, our knowledge of him ceases. It remains clear that he, more than anyone else the family had produced to that time, was a person of serious scholarly tastes and capabilities, of wide intellectual interests, and of exceptional promise an educator, perhaps also as a thinker of his time. I see no single tragedy in the family's history greater, then or since, than his untimely death. And there could have been no finer obituary tribute to his qualities than some words spoken, exactly a half a century after his death, by one of the other three who had shared with him entry as a student at the University of Vermont in 1812. These words were spoken at an alumni gathering in Burlington, in 1852, by one Charles Adams, Esq., of that place.

"There were four of us," Mr. Adams said,

who graduated fifty years ago. Three are present on this occasion. The joy of our meeting is chastened by the reflection that our other classmate, Jairus Kennan, is no more. He was feeble while in college, and having long struggled with disease, has gone, as we trust, to a higher and better world. Jairus Kennan was not an ordinary man. He loved knowledge, and nothing could repress his ardor in the pursuit. His intellectual powers were of a high order, and he cultivated them with untiring devotion. He was distinguished for warmth of feeling and kindness of manner, and had he lived, would have taken high rank as a philanthropist. Poor in purse and poorer in health, he was above adverse circumstances.

Mary (Tullar) Kennan.

George Kennan, father of
Thomas L. Kennan.

FIVE

Far-Northern New York

he experiences of the older brother of the unfortunate Jairus, Thomas, in the first years of the family's residence in Waterbury were mentioned in the last chapter. They included, it will be recalled, his marriage, very soon after the arrival of the family, to one Sally Lathrop and the birth of their first child, George—all in 1795. These years also included his turning to religion, his collaboration in the establishment of a Congregational church in Waterbury (meaning a formally organized congregation, but this in the absence of any church structure), and his baptism and pastoral ordination around the turn of the century. Because he was the one of the brothers to whom it fell to constitute the next generational link in the family line we are here pursuing, his later life must now be examined in greater detail.

Here, once more, as in the case of Thomas's mother, Abigail, the historian is frustrated by the utter absence of any personal detail about either him or his wife. Again: not a personal document, not a quoted oral phrase, not a letter or a critical comment. What they *did* can be painstakingly reconstructed; what they *were* remains concealed. There is, to be sure, a very impressive photograph of father Thomas, in his old age, and to this we may return later; but it tells us very little about the young man and his young wife who, as we resume the story, were just in process of leaving Vermont, and, as it turned out, for good.

Returning briefly to those first years of the family's life in Waterbury (actually, the last years of the eighteenth century), we should note that little George, born in 1795, was not the only one of the children of Thomas and Sally Kennan born in that place in just those years. There was another Abigail, born in 1797; a little son, Thomas, born in 1799; and another child, Clarissa, who appeared in 1801, just at the time when the father was assisting in the creation of the Waterbury Congregational church. And one finds oneself wondering whether this abundance of children in the Thomas Kennan family might not have had something to do with the complete and final removal of that family from the Waterbury region in the years 1802 to 1806. For mother Abigail, with a husband and one or two children of her own to accommodate in the primitive log house that was now also to be used as an inn, might well have rebelled at the prospect of housing a further family already consisting by 1801 of six human beings, and with more in prospect.

In any case, Thomas's ordination, coming on top of this family situation, confronted him with the necessity of finding some new and reasonably remunerative employment of his energies over the period immediately before him. The problem seems to have been momentarily relieved by a short term of service as a substitute pastor in the neighboring town of Stowe (the present ski resort); and this may have tidied things over in the years 1803–1805. But the question then arises: why did he not seek a regular pulpit somewhere else in Vermont?

To this, again, there is of course no answer. But this was a time when the two schools of Vermont Presbyterianism were locked in bitter conflict over the Great Awakening. And one of the positions of the strictly Calvinistic conservative faction was that no one who had not had some form of formal academic training in the field of theology ought to be considered eligible for a pastoral position. Thomas Kennan, of course, lacked any such training. So it would not have been in any way surprising had the influence of this powerful faction been brought to bear against his being given any pulpit within the state of Vermont.

In any case, the next thing we find (and this, again, without explanation) is the family packing up, leaving Vermont altogether, and moving to a small rural district in north-central New York. There they seem to have settled somewhere in the vicinity of two hamlets, spaced about five miles apart, bearing the names of Moira and Bangor. But what brought them there, where, specifically, they lived, and what the father was doing to support the family over the period of some twelve years that they appear to have lived there—all these questions remain to be examined.

And so dense is the obscurity that the historian is tempted to throw up his hands and say that the problem is insoluble on available evidence. But he does not have that privilege.

What we are confronted with here, nearly two centuries in the past, is mystery. And in the effort to solve the mystery, the historian can only fall back on the favored devices of the detective story writer: first, the *exclusion* of the wilder and more absurd hypotheses, and second, the patient pursuit and *inclusion* of such shreds of circumstantial evidence as can be unearthed. We shall see whether, with the help of these devices, this historian cannot discern at least the bare outlines of what became of the family over the twelve years in question.

Let us start with a major exclusion. My grandfather was under the impression, as reflected in his book, that the purpose of the family's move to this region of northern New York was to enable Thomas to take up, in a town called Moira, the duties of a Presbyterian pastor.

Well, there are very few certainties about the fate of the family at that time; but one of them is that Grand-father, in entertaining that impression, was seriously in error. This was at that time still frontier country. Moira was a tiny frontier settlement, even younger than Waterbury. The log cabins of the first two settlers had been built and occupied only two or three years before the Kennans came onto the scene. The place was not to be officially recognized as a town until 1828. The first Presbyterian church was established there in 1823. And there is not the faintest evidence that the Thomas Kennans ever lived in that village itself. It is possible that Grandfather, writing some eighty years later, was misled by learning that when a Congrega-tional church *was* finally established there, in 1823, its first pastor was one *John* Kennan. This could not pos-sibly have been either Thomas or his son John. It was most probably a grandson of one of Thomas's uncles.

A similar situation appears to have prevailed, at

least initially, in the case of the other of the two villages, Bangor. Here, too, the establishment of a regular church with a regular pastor was some twenty years in the future.

If, then, our Kennans did not settle in either of the two hamlets just mentioned, where *could* they have settled? To this question there is only one answer: at some place in the surrounding countryside. But what, then, could they have been doing there? Again, there is only one answer: primarily farming. Such was the state of development of the region at that time that the countryside adjacent to the two villages offered no other occupation.

Nor was it strange that Thomas, even as a newly ordained minister, should have turned, at this point in his career, to agriculture as at least a partial means of supporting a growing family at a time when no other immediate possibility presented itself. Farming, after all, was in the family tradition. He himself had been brought up, albeit as a small boy, on the farm near Charlemont. Farming was, in any case, for him a natural thing to fall back on.

And there must have been some encouragement in that direction from the New York end. No one in his right mind, and especially no one with a wife and several very small children in tow, would have set forth on such a move at random without having some idea of where he was to live, with what he was to occupy himself, and how he was to support the family in the process. There must have been some sort of an encouraging offer or invitation at the New York end. And this must have included a plot of ground and a habitation on which the Kennans could hope to settle.

And from whom could such a communication have come? Again, no answer.

But before we go further to explore what Thomas *might* have been doing in this new life, there are one or two background factors that could usefully be borne in mind.

We might note, first, that the term "church" did not necessarily mean, in the usage of that day, a formally established religious community disposing over a special church structure and functioning under the leadership and guidance of a regular, full-time pastor. It was quite possible for a group of people of common denominational persuasion in a given village to convene and to constitute themselves a "church" forthwith, even though no pastor had as yet been suggested and appointed. That young Thomas was fully familiar with this situation is evidenced by the fact that it was he himself who had acted as recording secretary for a gathering of just this sort shortly before he left Waterbury.

And secondly, even if and when a pastor had been "called" and had agreed to serve in that capacity, this did not mean that he had to be a resident of the immediate community, to hold regular Sabbath services there, or to restrict his services to that single community. There was in fact a very considerable degree of flexibility in the relations between pastor and flock in those small frontier communities.

We ought perhaps also to recall that even though Thomas did not at that time hold a regular pastoral position in either of the two hamlets, this did not preclude using his ministerial status in other ways by contributing to the religious needs of the surrounding rural population. There were occasions in the lives of the most primitive frontier families, and particularly the great solemn and sometimes even tragic moments such as marriages, baptisms, grave illness, funerals, and burials, which required the presence and the authority of a qualified minister of the gospel. And, Thomas's ministerial qualifications being widely known (as they were bound to be), there would have been nothing unnatural in his services being occasionally called upon, and not just by Presbyterians, for such occasions.

Nor would the religious field necessarily have been the only way that Thomas could find usefulness in the surrounding community beyond the limits of his own farm. There was also the field of education.

The first rural school in the area around Moira was founded in 1806, just around the time the Kennans were arriving in that vicinity. And the evidence shows it to have been situated (on a road, surely) somewhere between the two villages of Moira and Bangor. What could have been more natural than that Thomas and/or his wife should be drawn into its activities? They were, after all, in all probability the best-educated people in the vicinity.

There is another reason, too, why this possibility has to be considered. And that lies in what we know of the unusually high educational level of the children of Thomas and Sally Kennan. Three of these children went on to study at the St. Lawrence Academy in Potsdam, New York, not very far from where the Kennans were presumably living. That academy, although then only recently founded, appears to have been an excellent institution by the standards of that day or, at least in part (allowing for the great environmental changes) by those of any other day. Its curriculum of that time might perhaps be regarded as roughly comparable to the senior high school and junior college levels of our own time. The students (relatively few at that time) lived in the main academy building and were held, during term, under strict disciplinary control.

That the Kennan children were admitted to this academy and acquitted themselves creditably as students there seems to me to speak for the high quality of both the grammar-school teaching and of the home tutoring by which it must have been preceded. And both of those considerations speak, in my view, for the likelihood that the father was involved at both levels.

And there was another factor, too, that deserves attention in that connection.

When the Kennan family moved to upper New York, they presumably passed through Plattsburgh, on the western shore of Lake Champlain, at that time the greatest town of the entire region and certainly its leading Presbyterian center. And if so, they would have met, and indeed probably have been received by, the greatly respected long-term Presbyterian pastor in that city, the Rev. Frederick Halsey. He had occupied that pastorate since 1796, and was, at the time the Kennans passed through Plattsburg, approaching retirement; but he was still the leading Presbyterian pastor in the region and took a keen interest in the churches of that denomination that were springing up across it. And in 1814, some years after the movements of the Kennans to the region, he took the lead in establishing, at Plattsburg, the first presbytery, or unifying body, for those churches. As founded, this body included Halsey himself, as chairman, and some five or six other ministers from churches across the region. In the following year, the presbytery, acting surely with the authority of the next-higher body, the synod, elected Thomas Kennan as the first of its nonfounding members. This was the very year of Halsey's retirement, but there can be no question that the decision to appoint Kennan had his approval, if it was not indeed the result of his initiative. It shows clearly that Kennan, although not the "settled" pastor of any of the still only partially organized Presbyterian groups in the two villages, was a well-known and respected figure in that part of the country.

For information about the Rev. Thomas Halsey and the Champlain Presbytery (as the one in Plattsburgh was generally called) I am, incidentally, greatly and exclusively indebted to Mary Hutchins Lindow, a retired teacher in Clarke County in central Wisconsin. Mrs. Lindow is the author and compiler of an extraordinary fine privately printed genealogical study entitled *Lest We Forget our Pioneer Heritage.* The study is devoted primarily to the history of her own Hutchins family, but it includes several pages of excellently researched material about the Kennans (the two families having been joined many years ago by the marriage of a granddaughter of Thomas Kennan to Lyman Hutchins of Macomb, New York). Mrs. Lindow's careful eye had discovered what mine had not: that Hurd's *History of Clinton and Franklin Counties* (New York, 1850) contained a brief article on Thomas Halsey accompanied, although very inconspicuously at a lower corner of the page, by a list of the members of the Champlain Presbytery. Here, immediately after the names of the founding members, comes this entry:

"Reverend Thomas Kennan, 1815, Bangor, received."
(The "received" meant already ordained, "1815" the
date of his acceptance as a member of the presbytery.)

It is characteristic of the trials of a family historian
that these few words threw a greater and clearer light
on the nature of Thomas's life and work in his ten to
fifteen years of residence in northern New York than
all the rest of the relevant information I had been able
to gather.

For the author of the note on Thomas Halsey in the
volume just mentioned added the following about that
gentleman's retirement: "He retired to a farm upon the
outskirts of the village, and besides cultivating it,
taught school both at the academy and at his home
and supplied the pulpits of neighboring churches."

Could there have been any better and closer
description than this of the probable situation and
occupation of Thomas Kennan in his years of residence in that part of the country?

All this leads one to wonder whether it was not perhaps Halsey who had made the arrangements for the
residence of Kennan and his family in the Moira-
Bangor area, and had issued the corresponding invitation to them to make the move. Here, too, it is perhaps
worth noting that faced with the tense conflict of
the time between the Old School and the New within the Presbyterian denomination, the Champlain
Presbytery, like Kennan himself, inclined strongly to
the New School persuasion; and there must have been
for Halsey a not inconsiderable incentive for the introduction into the region, and in a sense the promotion,
the elevation into the presbytery, of a younger clergy-
man of this same persuasion.

The reader will note that in the listing just cited,

Bangor was shown as the seat of Kennan's position as minister. That did not mean, of course, that the village of Bangor was necessarily Kennan's place of residence. It could have meant anywhere in the vicinity of the village. But there are other reasons to suppose that in the final years of the residence of the Kennan family in that area, the connections with Bangor were closer than those with Moira. And for one indication of this we may turn now to the person of the oldest son of Thomas and Sally: by name, George.

George differed greatly from his younger brothers in that he was not only no intellectual but was a devoted farmer, then and thereafter over the remaining years of his life. Only ten or eleven years old when the family moved to New York, he matured physically over the years of its residence there. And he must have been a great source of strength for the father in combining agriculture with wider concerns.

We now find George marrying in "Bangor," on February 20, 1817, a girl who had been brought up there (and probably in the village itself), one Mary Tullar. And it was none other than George's father, Thomas, who conducted the wedding ceremony.

Mary's father was a farmer, again of Vermont origin, known in the locality as Captain Chester Tullar (the title acquired by service in the New York militia). Her mother was one Eudotia (Cooke) Tullar. The Tullar family had moved to Bangor in 1806—about the same time as the Kennan family had made its move to that vicinity. And the Tullar daughter Mary, a small child when the move was made, had grown up and received her schooling in Bangor village or its surroundings. She was, even at the young age of her marriage, a woman of firm and strong character. Her

parents were Baptists. It was in that denomination
that Mary was reared. She never wavered in this commitment, and she moved her young husband to join
her in it.

The marriage of George and Mary was followed,
less than two years later, by the move of the remainder
of the family to a town some thirty-five to forty miles
southwest of Bangor, where father Thomas was to
take up a much more regular pastorate. (About all
that—anon.) But George and Mary did not immediately accompany them on that move. They continued
for some years to reside on the farm where the family
had presumably lived for more than a decade, somewhere in the neighborhood of the two villages. And
only at a later date did George and Mary move to the
region of New York state where the father had by this
time settled, and where, only a few miles away, he,
George, had acquired a farm of his own and had built,
with his own hands, a house to accommodate the
farmer.

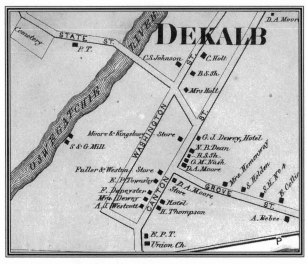

Map of DeKalb, New York, c. 1820s.

SIX

DeKalb

n the year 1819, less than two years after his officiation at the marriage of his son George in Bangor, Thomas Kennan, accompanied by as much of the family as had remained with the parents, moved from the Moira-Bangor vicinity to a region some thirty-five to forty miles to the southwest, specifically to a small New York town or village called DeKalb. There he was to serve for some thirteen years (and this for the first and last time in his life) as a "settled" pastor—the minister, to be exact, of DeKalb's first Presbyterian church.

Of all of this—of what brought him to make this move, of how he and his wife lived over those ensuing years, of his experiences as a pastor, and of the tenor of his preachings—we have, as for so many other aspects of the lives of those first three American Kennan generations, no documentary or other firsthand evidences. I have no doubt that with careful study of the circumstantial evidence, as was applied in the last of these chapters, more could be brought to light on these uncertainties. But here, for the first time, I find

The children of Rev. Thomas Kennan. The two sons, John (left)
and Jairus (right), stand at the ends of the top row.
The three sisters sit in the center of the second row.

myself confronted seriously with the question: would
the effort be worthwhile?

We have seen that from the standpoint of family
history the most remarkable feature of the life of
Thomas Kennan and his wife, Sally, was the effort
they put forward to give their children a proper childhood rearing and, where practical, education. And this
would be only one more instance, out of a myriad of

Each Kennan has his or her spouse alongside him or her,
except for the central sister, whose husband stands above her.
The photo was taken in the 1850s.

others, in which the quality of the children was
achieved largely by the self-effacement of the parents.
With the completion of this effort, the focus of attention of the family historian tends to move from the
parents to the children.

To recognize this last is not to claim that the children of Thomas and Sally were particularly remarkable people, or that they all had brilliant careers in the

eyes of the American society of their time. The only one of their progeny who won any wide public recognition was not a son but a grandson born in Norwalk, Ohio. But fame, after all, was never the highest criterion of human quality. What Thomas and Sally clearly achieved was to produce, for the most part, a family of a considerably higher intellectual and cultural quality than the ones they had known in their own childhoods, and to assure, by that generational change, the transition from a farming-colonial culture to one more in keeping with the natural aptitudes of the persons in question and with the standards of the more widely developing American society of their time.

In the light of those observations, this might be a good point to reproduce, for the reader's edification, the first photograph ever made of any group—three daughters and two sons—of the children of Thomas and Sally, each accompanied by and seated next to (in one instance below) his or her spouse.

(It would be interesting to know when and where this picture was taken. The ages of the children suggest that it could not have been much earlier than 1848 or later than 1855. And the place? Perhaps Ogdensburg, New York.)

In any case, there they all are, photographed in middle age, long after the deaths of their parents. And each reader will have his own impression of what the picture suggests. To me, it is a well-ordered and cohesive family circle, composed of strong, remarkably healthy, intelligent, well-educated, and self-respecting people. The term "well-educated" should be taken, of course, in the relative sense. The only ones who had had higher education were, of course, the daughter Philena, who, although ending as a farmer's wife like the others, had attended the St. Lawrence Academy and had herself taught school, and then the two sons: John, the oldest of the lot, shown standing at the left end of the top row in the picture, the beneficiary of at least three years of attendance at Hamilton College, himself something of an educator, and father of the widely known explorer, writer, and authority on Russia George Kennan (1845–1924); and, at the other end of that top row, Jairus, the youngest of the lot, and, by the time the picture was taken, a successful and highly respected attorney in Norwalk, Ohio.

We do not know, as was noted above, what lay behind Thomas's decision to move to DeKalb. All we know is that the decision to make the move was not hastily taken. It was definitely planned and arranged at least a year in advance. That fact is not, in itself, of any great importance. But the source from which our information about it is derived is revealing with relation not only to Thomas's generation but to an earlier stage in the family's history as well.

When Thomas and Sally made the move to northern New York, they left behind in Waterbury Thomas's own father and mother. Waterbury grew, with impressive rapidity, from the original small forest settlement the Kennans had known at the time of their arrival there to the dimensions of a sizable and well-recognized small town. And it was there, plainly, that they continued to live after the son and family moved to New York. For some years, as noted in the chapter on Waterbury, father George took an active part in the local governmental affairs of that community. And indeed as late as 1808 he was still representing the town, from time to time, in the Vermont assembly. But by 1816, being now in his sixties, he seems to have retired into private affairs, and not very remunerative ones at that. He was at that time, it might also be noted, the only one of our line of the family whose memories reached back over the entire range of the family's life and places of residence, beginning with the first generation's residence in Holden, Massachusetts. There is no evidence, however, that he ever received any formal education beyond whatever grammar school instruction Holden might have given him.

In the first years after the removal of Thomas and his family to New York, there appears to have been no communication between the families of father and son. But in the three and a half years beginning July 1816 and ending January 1820, father George wrote four letters to his son Thomas; and these survived, to rest peacefully for nearly a hundred years among Grandfather's papers. I have them now before me— the only written words ever bequeathed to posterity by any member of those three family generations. They are, characteristically, the letters of an old man, tired, unhappy, sometimes complaining, and a poorly educated old man at that. Each of them contains multiple misspellings—some of them amusingly phonetic in inspiration. Punctuation is notable for its almost total absence. The letters begin, routinely, with wishes for good health and with comments on the health of himself and those about him, and they end with similar passages.

It becomes evident, from the final letter of January 29, 1820, that son Thomas, now already planning to move to a part of New York even farther from Waterbury than Bangor, had recently paid a last (summer of 1819) and only filial visit to Waterbury. One may suppose that the main purpose of this visit was to see, once more, the mother. The earlier letters contain no reference to her. But this last letter, written about half a year after Thomas's visit, ends with a postscript to the effect that "your Mom sends her love to you and all the children. Do right [i.e., write] as often as you can and let us know your well."

The letters are interesting, too, for one inference they invite. Abigail, whose modest name appears nowhere in the documentation of those first years of the nineteenth century, was plainly and naturally continuing to live with her husband when these four letters were written; and she must, one supposes, have seen them before they were dispatched. In the circumstances, they would scarcely have been written behind her back. Yet it would appear that she allowed them to be sent without any effort on her part to correct the numerous misspellings and grammatical mistakes. Did this mean that despite having well-educated forebears, as we have seen, she was herself very poorly educated, much more poorly than her daughter-in-law Sally? Probably, one must suppose. But could it not also have been that Abigail, who had seen much, endured much, and expended much of herself in the forty-seven years of her marriage, had simply "had it" and just didn't greatly care anymore? She died, it appears, shortly thereafter.

But back, now, to Thomas and his DeKalb pastorship.

Thomas Kennan must have arrived in DeKalb in late 1819 and have taken over almost at once his position as minister to the first Presbyterian church in that vicinity. The church community that awaited his arrival had, at that time, no actual church structure of its own. Like so many other communities of that sort in that region, its members came together periodically in whatever premises could be made available, often a schoolhouse or a barn. But even for this, they required a pastor; and it was thus that Thomas must initially have served. A regular church structure was erected in 1823, four years after his arrival, and it was surely there for ten further years, that he conducted services.

But beyond the bare fact that he was there and was occupying that position, we *know*, in the strict meaning of that term, nothing. Where he lived, how often he preached, what sort of a congregation sat before him, and what sort of sermons he delivered—of all this we simply have no knowledge. We are left, as so often in this inquiry, to consult the known surrounding circumstances, the probabilities, and our own imaginations.

The horizon of any Presbyterian pastor serving in that place at that time can only have been greatly darkened by awareness of the increasing intensity of the conflict between the Old School and New within the Presbyterian community. Thomas Kennan, like many others of the Presbyterian pastors of the region, must have been well aware of where the conflict was heading during the years of his pastorate, and what did indeed come to pass very shortly after he left that position. This was a complete break between the two factions, placing them out of all contact with each other for many years to come. And he must have perceived that such a break threatened the entire future of the Presbyterian Church in America. For us, it might therefore be justifiable to take a closer look, at this point, at the nature of the conflict.

At the heart of the Old School attitudes lay what

people believed to be Calvinist doctrine. Now, far be it from me to attempt to summarize in a few words what that doctrine was. (My own impression is that Calvin was himself a sadly confused man, doing an endless and tortuous battle with the contradictions inherent in his own professed convictions. He was thus inclined to confuse, and did confuse, a great number of other people.) More important, however, is what people of the time we are examining may have thought his doctrine to be. This, too, is greatly uncertain and was probably not exactly the same in the eyes of any two individuals. But it might, I should think, have been something like this: that the great mass of Christian believers shared, indeed could not help but share, the guilt for Adam's sin, were hopelessly corrupted by it, and were therefore in a state of total depravity; and that they, as such, could not expect to be the beneficiaries of the grace of God. Exceptions to this harsh judgment and tragic fate were to be only, it seems, the members of a small spiritual elite, selected, we are told, by God, but made evident to the fortunate subjects only by some mysterious inner awareness on their own part.

Crude and approximate as these assumptions may be, it takes little imagination to perceive that such teachings were not greatly helpful to the average frontier-village pastor. He stood, after all, at the very heart of the lives of his flock. He was obliged to be present, and to assist at, the most crucial events of those lives: the births, the baptisms, the confirmations, the marriages, the illnesses, the funerals and burials. He had to see his people through the manifold injustices and cruelties inflicted by nature and sheer chance: the seemingly senseless accidents, the

fatal illnesses of little children, and the ravages of con-
tagious disease. His duties required him to support
daily, and to ask his parishioners to support, charity
over cruelty, generosity over meanness, faith over cynicism. He had, in short, to sustain the faith of his fol-
lowers in God's justice and compassion. And in all of
this, the despairing extremisms of Calvinist philoso-
phy were of little use to him.

And so the differences between the two "schools"
flourished and rankled. What, for example, should be
the relationship of Presbyterian pastors to their col-
leagues of other denominations? "Have nothing to do
with them," the Old School would have said. "They
are doctrinally pernicious. We alone are the possessors
of the truth." The New School, of course, disagreed.
There were fields of activity, they thought, where they
might usefully merge their efforts with those of people of other doctrinal or denominational commitment. All of them, after all, worshiped the same God.
Intolerant feuding among Christians could, in their
view, only weaken the Christian cause.

And what, spokesmen of the New School would
have asked, about missionary work? Their own local
resources were too slender to permit them to go far
alone along that path. Were there not here, too, possibilities and even necessities for association with others? Again, the Old School disapproved.

The Old School, as we have already had opportunity to note, held that the pastoral clergy should be
limited to men who had had formal theological training in some suitable institution. "No," the New School
would have said, "you cannot find enough of such people at this juncture. New churches are springing up all
over the region. There is already a shortage of pastors.

Better a young one who, poorly educated as he might be in your view, might at least communicate to others something of the power and conviction of his own faith, than no pastor at all, or one who speaks, intellectually, over the heads of his flock."

Thomas Kennan was known as an adherent to the New School. It is improbable that this caused him any personal difficulty. This was the persuasion of the great bulk of Presbyterian clergy of the region he inhabited, including the members of the presbytery to which he now belonged. But the whole conflict must have worried him with the threat it posed for the future of the denomination of his commitment. And I find myself wondering whether this, the impending split in the Presbyterian church, did not have something to do, even if it was not the only reason, for his retirement in the year 1833 from his position as minister, and indeed from all further formal religious activity.

A lesser but not wholly insignificant burden on Thomas's life as a pastor may well have been the vigor, at just that time, of the movement known as revivalism. It had its origins, as I understand it, in the impression obtained by some younger members of the clergy of northeastern New England and New York that Christian teaching in the Protestant churches of that entire region had seriously sagged down, and had lost its vitality, emotional intensity, and immediacy in the lives of the parishioners. This situation, in their view, called for correction; and this, they believed, could be given to it if they were to break away from the ranks of the regular clergy and sally forth on their own as itinerant evangelists, visiting not only one religious community but as many as possible, and conveying directly, to such groups of listeners as could be assembled, their message of the burning realities, as they saw them, of sin, repentance, and God's grace. In carrying this message forward they seem to have avoided theological and even denominational distinctions. Their appeal was primitive, emotional, stark, and simple. It was aimed directly at the consciences of individual listeners. The latter were enjoined to search their memories for instances of particular sinfulness in their own lives, sinfulness previously hidden from others, and sometimes even from themselves, and to confess openly, before such audiences as the revivalist had contrived to bring together, the shocking dimensions of their sins and the agonizing depths of their repentance. If they did all this, there would be, they were assured, a chance of their being "born again," starting a new and hopeful life, and of thus becoming the beneficiaries of God's grace. If they failed to do so, their souls would be delivered, without possibility of redemption, into the hands of the Devil.

The gatherings to which such appeals were addressed were composed, for the most part, of very unsophisticated people. And this being the case, it is not surprising that the appeals evoked were often pathetic, dramatic, but highly hysterical. These sometimes took the form of moanings, groanings, sobbings, and even casting oneself onto the floor, in the agony of repentance. Such responses were then no doubt chalked up, on the revivalist's list, as evidences of further "souls saved."

Upon the regular settled pastors such activities imposed a number of burdens. There was, in the very appearance of one of the revivalists on the local scene, a rather subtle implication that the local pastor had not been doing his job very effectively. And there were sometimes even worse consequences of the revivalist's visit. Revivalists were known to leave behind them on many occasions a sad trail of psychic disorientation. As the effects of the hysteria began to fade, there was a tendency for it to be replaced by feelings of humiliation, by recognition of the ludicrous aspects of the subject's recent behavior, and how this must have appeared to others, with the result that in some instances the unfortunate subject, now confused and embittered, gave up churchgoing altogether.

These consequences, however, were not ones with which the revivalist had to deal. He, as a rule, was around the place for only a few days. It was left to the regular pastor to bear the burden of this trail of psychic devastation.

And it was not easy for him to protect himself from these visitors. The revivalist presented himself to the local community in the image of a devout Christian. He preached against sin and called for repentance. Well, what was the matter with that? He demanded submission to God's will. How could one oppose *that* without suggesting that he favored the defiance of that will?

The trouble was, of course, that the revivalist, having little to lose, tended to go at every point too far. Everyone, obviously, had *some* sins to repent. But, as I am sure the local pastor would have liked to point out, repentance did not need to take the form of hysterical dramatic performances in the presence of many other people. There were other ways of worshiping God and of recognizing one's own imperfections—ways that were (who knew?) possibly even more impressive in God's sight. But it is always difficult to deal, in any controversy, with the exaggerations of the other side without appearing to oppose the element of truth in what that side is arguing.

Whether Thomas Kennan suffered from such circumstances on other occasions we cannot know for sure. But there was one occasion on which he clearly did. And it is ironic that the account of it, as evidenced from the words of others, constitutes the nearest thing, on direct evidence, to a reflection of his pastorate.

In September 1825, at a point just about in the middle of Thomas's service as minister of the DeKalb church, there suddenly appeared on the local scene one of the youngest and most arresting of the revivalists, a certain Charles J. Finney. Born in Connecticut in the year 1792, Finney had been ordained as a minister only in 1824, barely a year before his visit to DeKalb. They both being in the formal sense Presbyterian pastors, and Kennan that of the only Presbyterian church in town, it may be supposed that Kennan would have been the first to receive Finney and to welcome him to that small community. Perhaps he tried to do so.

A few years ago there was published, in Grand Rapids, Michigan, a hefty and well-annotated volume of Finney's memoirs. They included an entire chapter on his visit to DeKalb, which he seems to have regarded as one of the greatest triumphs of his evangelistic career.

"Here," wrote Finney at the outset of this chapter, "was a Presbyterian church and minister; but the church was small, and the minister seemed not to have a very strong hold upon the people. However, I think he was decidedly a good man."

So far, so good. But a footnote to that page describes another incident that leaves a quite different impression. Another person who talked with Finney, apparently on that same day, found the latter under the impression that Kennan's name was Cannon, and quoted him as saying, obviously as a play on that name, that he, Finney, would "either make him [this cannon] roar or would spike him."

It might be worth recalling that the man Mr. Finney was proposing to treat in this manner was his senior by seventeen years in age, and by twenty-four years in ecclesiastical experience.

How happy or unhappy for Thomas Kennan were those years of pastoral service in DeKalb we have no means of knowing. He and his wife, Sally, must, in any case, have derived happiness and pride from the spectacle of the successful progress in the education of the three of their children whose paths led in the direction of higher studies. Two of them, John and his sister Philena, were in just those years students at the St. Lawrence Academy; and it was within the same time frame that John went on to further study at Hamilton College. Meanwhile the youngest son, Jairus, was, when his father's pastorship ended, just on the point of following in the footsteps of his two siblings.

But all things must have their ending; and so, at the beginning of the third decade of that century, did the career of Thomas Kennan. On July 18, 1831, his wife, Sally, died. Left, now, an elderly bachelor, devoid of the intimate companionship that had supported him over so many years, he terminated his pastorship and moved, plainly in response to the invitation of his son John, to Norwalk, Ohio, to which place the son had by now moved. There, we are told, Thomas kept a horse and wagon and a plot of land in the country, beyond the town. And this he seems to have tilled with his own hands. (One sees that, alongside the pastor, the farmer in the end claimed his own.) After some ten years of this retirement, Thomas Kennan died, in Norwalk, on the 26th of July, 1843. With his death, the history of the first three American generations of the family finds its ending.

It would be wrong, however, to conclude this chapter without a word about Thomas's person. To give that word is not an easy task. The nearest thing we have in the way of direct evidence is a photograph, produced, surely, in Norwalk, and probably not long before he died.

We know from other evidence, of course, that he was a faithful and devoted husband and father—a man with a high sense of honor and duty—a man whom contemporary members of the family should be proud to recognize as their real patriarch. And the photograph reveals him, beyond that, as a man of firm principle, who, as farmer, as pastor, and as a father and grandfather, had seen a great deal of the good and the bad in humankind and had come through it all with his beliefs, his principles, and his capacities for both severity and gentleness unscathed. If the biblical injunction to "honor thy father and mother" can be extended to include those whom those parents in turn were enjoined to honor, then this Thomas, my grandfather's grandfather, may properly be included within the scope of that injunction.

Thomas Kennan in his old age,
presumably around the year 1840.

Grandfather George Kennan's cabin.

Epilogue

his concludes what I picture to myself as the innocent stage in the Kennan family's history. It was innocent mainly in the sense that it involved no residence in any large urban community. The normal occupation of the first three generations of the family in America was farming. (Something of the taste for growing things was destined to mark most of the male family members even into later times.) It was, then, essentially a country or village life that these early Kennans lived. The association with crops and animals, and the struggle against the recalcitrance of nature in the face of human demands: these were the predominant realities and challenges the family had to confront.

This mode of life, centered around the small single-family farm, was of course far from being idyllic. The physical labor it imposed was wearing and usually monotonous. On the younger members of the family, in particular, it imposed burdens that to them often seemed stultifying and unreasonable. For many of these youngsters, influenced by such smattering glimpses as were available to them of the world out-side, almost any other mode of life seemed preferable to farming. I can recall my father, who had been brought up on a farm, saying to me: "George, never, never be a farmer. It's the damnedest drudgery you can imagine." (And this from a man who, in later life, loved vegetable gardening, though not as a way of life.)

On the other hand, this institution of the small family farm, as the early Kennans knew it, had much to be said for it. It bred, or tended to breed, strong peo-ple—strong both physically and emotionally. It effec-tively ruled out for married couples the escape hatches of separation and divorce; and in this way it encour-aged the cohesion of the family. If it discouraged, as it plainly did, flights of speculation on more abstract and theoretical questions, and could thus be seen as restricting intellectual development, it engendered, in place of all this, a certain simplicity and practicality of outlook and expression that had its own charm and eloquence, contrasting favorably with most of the arti-ficialities of urban culture. It left enduring marks on succeeding generations, and not in New England alone. Beyond which, the inescapable discipline of the small family farm inculcated in its devotees certain qualities of self-reliance, independence, individual responsibility, and pride of landownership that played a unique role in the shaping of character. But because these positive aspects of the farmer's life tended to be more pronounced among the older members of the family than among the younger ones, they tended to produce in a great many farm households a genera-tional tension that was hard on both parties.

What has just been described was a form of life pursued in all the rural-agricultural areas (which meant by far the preponderant areas) of the New England of that time. Thus the sparse glimpses this account has given us of the life of these Kennans was revealing for something far wider and more important than the experiences of any single family: namely, the regional culture of all rural New England. It was a culture that had its roots in those regions of the British Isles from which, almost exclusively, the first family immigrants were drawn. These were the predominantly Protestant regions of northern England and southern Scotland. And it was from these sources that there were drawn the essential features of the regional culture: the social customs, the domestic habits, the civil-political concepts, and above all the religious commitments of the great body of New Englanders. And these features retained their defining power over much of New England culture long beyond the decades treated in this narrative—in part, indeed, down to the present day.

Of all of this the Kennans, in most respects an unexceptional family of their time and place, had their share. And they were, in this sense, full-fledged New Englanders. If they were in any way atypical of the rest of New England, this lay only in the remoteness of their various residences from the few urban centers, beginning, of course, with Boston, of the remainder of New England. One finds in the life of this family almost no evidence of the influences of any of these major urban centers. It is a striking fact that over all the seven or eight decades of its life in that northern region there appears to have been only one instance of any member of the family visiting or even seeing any sizable urban center; this instance was the brief visit to New York by Jairus Kennan shortly before his death.

For the rest, the Kennans were the epitome of the back-country family of the most remote northern fringes of New England life.

There was, however, another minor aspect of atypicality that set this family off even from their neighbors in this far-northern region. And this was something that lay in what might be called the atmosphere of the home. For there is every evidence that in the second and third generations of the family this atmosphere was flowing from the exactly opposite geographical end of New England from the northern frontiers where the Kennans lived, namely the southern and southwestern districts of Connecticut. And in both instances, the two mothers, Abigail Sherman and Sally Lathrop (by maiden names), both exceptionally fine and strong persons, were by family tradition and personal upbringing Connecticut women. They were steeped in the customs and outlooks of a part of New England older, more mature, and educationally more highly developed than anything that the Holdens, Charlemonts, Waterburys, or Bangors of that time had to offer.

These instances of what I have called "atypicality" in the Kennan family were ones related to the times and places of the family's residence. But there was one further abnormality that not only set these Kennans off from their surroundings of that time but was destined to pursue them, as a family, into later decades as well. This was their persistent, and apparently compulsive, striving for maximum independence in both their personal and social lives. This was a characteristic that seems to have affected primarily the male family members; and I suspect that it was one inherited from their Scottish ancestors but destined to be passed on from father to son as long, down to the present, as the family was known under the name of Kennan.

Now, extreme personal independence of this sort implied and demanded, of course, the forfeiture of such support as could have been had from closer association, commercial, professional, social, or what you will, with others. The Kennans, I suspect, understood this and accepted it. And it was, in these circumstances, not surprising that when these and members of later generations of the family turned to the problem of selecting long-term professional involvements, it was to what might be called the lonely ones—the farm, the law, the pulpit, the pen, and the scholar's dedication—that they gave precedence. These callings, whatever their implicit burdens, presented a measure of defense against interference or domination from outside.

I cannot end this review of the lives of these first three generations of the American Kennan family without a word of deeply felt tribute to the three sets of parents who presided over its affairs.

The body of these three generations of the family, including the parents and those of the children who survived the childhood diseases, numbered, as the Russians would have put it, twenty-eight souls. Reviewing what I know of their lives, I cannot find in them any instances of deviousness, sordidness, or cynicism. They seemed all to have been "whole" persons, content with their background, afflicted with feelings of neither inferiority nor of superiority vis-à-vis others, pretending to be nothing other than what they actually were. And trying to view them as individuals, I am unable to find among them a single weakling, a single physical invalid, a single crook, or a single villain.

At least a part of this relatively favorable situation was, it may be argued, the working of the law of chance. No doubt. But it could not have come into existence without the standards, the principles, and the guiding hands of the parents. All honor to them from this two-century distance!

*W*hat we have been talking about was, as we have seen, a subculture of the wider New England rural culture; and if one were to be asked to describe that subculture in terms of a single attribute, one would have to say that it was one of rural poverty. But the term "poverty" should not be seen here as a purely negative and regrettable feature of it. On the contrary, it was an essential part of it, in some respects perhaps regrettable, but without it the term "culture" would have lost all meaning.

Not even in the highly urbanized society of the American future would poverty always be recognized as a wholly negative component of life. Even there it would have its uses, if only as a threat, a challenge, and a conceivable punishment for failure. But how much greater and more positive was its role in relation to the single-family farm, where the hardship of it would be so immediately visible and where the task of combating it and holding it in check lay, barring extremely hard luck, at the very basis of the enterprise itself.

It must be emphasized that what these three generations of the Kennan family were involved in was not any organized community. It was a habitual way of life practiced by considerable bodies of people in various rural regions of New England where conditions for it seemed reasonably hospitable. Not only did it not require any particular organizational form, but its strength lay precisely in the absence of any organizational commitment—it was in the extensive independence of the very cells of which the farm was composed that its uniqueness resided. And left to itself, and viewed as a phenomenon within itself, this proved to be a strong and usually successful arrangement of human society, capable not only of maintaining a high level of human quality but of bequeathing that capability to its immediate posterity.

What better, then, than to have left it alone as it was (and this was the only demand it placed on its wider environment), protecting it in its isolation and consoling oneself that here, at least, was one theater of activity where quality in the individual human life was being humanely and successfully pursued?

But it is at this point that we come up sharply against one insuperable obstacle that lay across such an approach. This was the double instability that marked this way of life—instability inherent within itself, and instability in its relation to surrounding environment.

The inherent instability was seated in two of the essential features of the lives of these people. One was religion; the other was education.

It is impossible even to conceive of farming life of this sort without the presence, and the major contribution, of the local church. Without the solaces it offered in times of tragedy; without its support through the harder passages of the professional struggle; without the solemnity it bestowed on the relations between parent and child; and without the hope it conveyed of favorable ultimate outcomes to the great mysteries of life and death—without these contributions from the church's side, it is hard to imagine how the lives in question could ever have been successfully conducted.

But the church itself was not an institution capable of existing in isolation. Such were not its origins. Such were not the limits of its dedication. It knew no geographic boundaries; and it could recognize no such limits to its concerns. It was a part of something vastly larger than any local scene. It remained perforce, whether one liked it or not, a link of great importance between the locality and the great world outside.

And education? Yes, if you will, it could be successfully imparted, in isolation, at the lowest level—the three R's. But the moment it rose above that, things were different. The moment teachers had to be brought in from the outside; the moment printed textbooks, prepared elsewhere, had to be imported and used; and the moment questions emerged among the pupils about life beyond the confines of the locality— the moment these things happened, the school became the outlet, and in a sense the introduction, to the wider world. The higher the educational aspirations of parents and pupils rose, the less these could be successfully met in conditions of complete local isolation.

And as for the pressures from outside, these presented themselves, of course, in a multitude of forms, almost all of them hostile, whether by intent or by unintended effect, to the maintenance of this single-farm culture. There seems to have been something inherent in American democracy, and particularly in that of the post-Federalist period, that made an ideal out of social and political uniformity, and had small tolerance for anything that challenged the wider patterns of democratic life that were emerging and deviated from that uniformity. This insistence on uniformity lay, in fact, at the heart of the American concept of government-by-law in preference to the wide latitude of local administrative discretion that a number of essentially democratic European societies permitted themselves. Law, after all, recognized no human impulses—no inherited standards, no preferences or aspirations—deviant from its letter. And this intolerance dominated not only existent judicial authority but very often the personal decisions of the lawmakers themselves, not to mention the tendencies of social and commercial circles across the nation.

There can be no question about it: the mainstream of American life resented and resisted all deviations, or even attempted deviations, from its uniformities. And if this required, as in most instances it surely did, the sacrifice of quality to quantity, so be it. Ours was to be a civilization of the least common denominator, to stand or fall with its requirements (as it was then about to do in the inflicting upon itself of the Civil War, and this, essentially, in the name of union and uniformity).

It was of course among the children of Thomas and Sally Kennan, and specifically with those who had the benefits of higher education, that the farming tradition of the Kennan family found its most significant ending. The ending cannot be said to have been a total and abrupt one. It was a gradual process. Several of the girls married farmers, and how many of the family's farming tendencies they carried with them we do not know. Beyond which there was the son George, a farmer by nature and by choice (and the only one of his generation, ironically, from whom I myself am directly descended)—a man who persisted in farming on relatively poor soil in the face of ferociously adverse weather conditions, and eventually suffered, but bore manfully, the almost inevitable hardships of failure.

But the fact remains: with the departure of the two well-educated sons, and their reestablishment in the relatively mature town of Norwalk, Ohio, where they pursued wholly nonagricultural careers, the farming tradition of the direct paternal line of the family found its final end.

Did the parents regret this? There is no sign that they did. They must have been well aware, as they pushed three of their children into higher education, that something like this would have to be the result. And there was now, for these latter, no turning back. They now owned no farm, anywhere. The single-family farm, as a way of life, as a source of the "daily bread," and in part (but only in part) as a culture, had found its ending in the church at DeKalb. And that, for the surviving children, was that!

$\mathcal{W}$as there any lasting meaning in the lives of these first three American generations of the Kennan family? If so, it was in their quality as New Englanders; for that, in the deepest sense, is what they were. At least 75 percent of the roots of Thomas and Sally's children reached back to the very earliest immigrants from among the Protestant-dissident peoples of northern England. The Scottish parental line supplied only the remaining 25 percent.

The Kennans must be seen then as only one tiny

component of the New England civilization of the seventeenth and eighteenth centuries. That this civilization was one of the leading determining elements in the American Revolution and in the organization and shaping of the national state to which it gave rise is clear. New England was also destined—alas—to play a somewhat diminished but nonetheless determining part in the unleashing of the immeasurable tragedy of the Civil War. Its relative importance as a factor in American life was even then being reduced over all the years of the eighteenth century by the huge quantities of immigrants of other cultures, other religion, and other tongues now flowing into the entire North American continent. Parts of these waves of immigration threatened to engulf New England itself, and to reduce its traditional culture to a subordinate position, even in the original homeland.

But a salient feature of New England's part in the shaping of modern American civilization, as it was in the eighteenth and early nineteenth centuries, has been not only in the contribution of that homeland, but also in that part of New England that emigrated to other regions, and notably across the Great Lakes to the region just beyond them. I am not a cultural historian, and would not wish to sound like one. But my own memories of Wisconsin, and particularly southern and central rural Wisconsin, recall a population deeply colored in habits, standards, and even speech by New England origins. And I am also moved to note that the families of my great-grandfather and his son, my grandfather, contributed to that state of affairs when they themselves moved, on the eve of the Civil War, to Green Bay and adjacent areas of Wisconsin.

Better historians than this one would have to supply the answer to this question; but I am moved to wonder whether, viewed in the long term, New England did not, in the nineteenth century, contribute as much to the national scene by what it exported of itself as by that part of it that was retained at home. If that is even the case, then it is a comfort for me to reflect that such modest contributions as the Kennan family may have been able to make to the substance of New England culture were directed both to what that culture was, for and in itself, and to that portion of it that found so congenial a new home for itself in my native state of Wisconsin.

ABOUT THE AUTHOR

*G*eorge F. Kennan has observed and commented on world affairs in newspapers, journals, and magazines, on radio, television, and in congressional testimony, with an insider's perspective and an outsider's freedom.

Kennan was trained as a Soviet specialist in the U. S. Foreign Service. In 1933 he accompanied William Bullitt, the first U. S. ambassador to the Soviet Union, becoming ambassador there himself in 1952. In 1947, Kennan became head of the State Department's first Policy Planning Staff, which became a primary influence in the formation of post–World War II foreign policy. On leaving Washington, D.C., in 1953, he became a scholar and professor at the Institute for Advanced Study in Princeton, and author of numerous works on diplomacy, history, foreign relations and policy, as well as major volumes of memoirs and reflections.

In addition to being a recipient of the Presidential Medal of Freedom, the founder of the Kennan Institute for Advanced Russian Studies in Washington, D.C., a past president of the American Academy of Arts and Letters and a recipient of its Gold Medal in History, Kennan has won, among other distinguished awards, two Pulitzer Prizes and a National Book Award.